COMMUNINGS
IN THE SANCTUARY

COMMUNINGS IN THE SANCTUARY

Robert Richardson

Introduced and Edited by C. Leonard Allen

NEW LEAF BOOKS
Orange, California

Portions of the Introduction are taken from Leonard Allen, *Distant Voices: Discovering a Forgotten Past for a Changing Church* (ACU Press, 1993). Used by permission.

ISBN 0–9700836–0–2

NEW LEAF BOOKS
12542 S. Fairmont
Orange, CA 92869

10 9 8 7 6 5 4 3 2 1

Table of Contents

Introduction

Robert Richardson (1806-1876) was one of the most gifted writers and finest theological minds in the first century of the Stone-Campbell movement. By training he was a medical doctor, but he spent much of his life teaching and working as an administrator at Bethany College in Bethany, West Virginia. He was an intimate friend of Alexander Campbell, serving as his family physician for over thirty years and as office manager and associate editor of Campbell's *Millennial Harbinger* for nearly thirty years.

When Campbell died in March of 1866, Dr. Richardson was the one chosen by the family to deliver the funeral sermon. He was also the one Campbell's family asked to write his biography. After three intense years of research and writing, Dr. Richardson completed the massive, two-volume *Memoirs of Alexander Campbell* in 1869, a work that remains today the major biography of Campbell.

"Out of the Cocoon of Formalism"

In a time of controversy and aggressive debating, Robert Richardson was unique in stressing the things of the Spirit and the devotional life. The debating mindset, he believed, produced a deadly spiritual vacuum. The effect of doctrinal controversy was to "distract the mind, destroy love, generate dislike, jealousy, revenge,

[and] foster the passions of the carnal nature." Too many people, he wrote, "are ready to argue, debate, discuss, at all times, . . . and will spend hours in the earnest defense of their favorite theories" but will not spend five minutes meditating "upon the character, the sayings, and perfections of Christ, or upon their own inward spiritual state."

Richardson believed that this was precisely the central problem with much of the Protestant world. Each Protestant sect had developed its distinctive doctrines and theories, encased them in creeds and confessions, then tenaciously defended them against all comers. In this way Protestantism had become one "grand doctrinal controversy." A grave error resulted, Richardson believed. Professed Christians began to mistake completely the nature and focus of the Christian faith. They began to view it "as a belief in doctrines; as consisting in correct intellectual views. . . ; as having respect to the mind rather than to the heart." More and more people came to regard "a correct view of doctrine as something absolutely essential to salvation, and as having in itself, if not a saving efficacy, at least a meritorious orthodoxy, which will go very far toward securing acceptance with God."

Richardson saw the same tendency in the Restoration movement. By the early 1840s he believed that a "heartless and superficial formalism" was overtaking the movement, and this conviction grew throughout the 1840s and 50s. He attributed this development, in large measure, to the clandestine influence of John Locke's philosophy. Locke was the premier English philosopher of the eighteenth century, and his influence was enormous in the young American nation. He taught that true knowledge can be gained only through the five senses and that human "reason must be our last judge and guide in everything."

Richardson labelled the popularized form of this philosophy the "dirt philosophy." He called it that because of its insistence that God could influence human beings only through material objects or through revealed words—no other way. Such a philosophy, he frequently charged, was spiritually debilitating, for it tends to "unfit men's minds to receive anything that is not merely outward and formal"; it thereby "gradually dries up the fountains of spiritual sympathy."

In a private letter to Isaac Errett on July 16, 1857, Richardson spoke to this point with unusual candor: "the philosophy of Locke with which Bro. Campbell's mind was deeply imbued in youth has insidiously mingled itself with almost all the great points in the reformation and has been all the while like an iceberg in the way — chilling the heart and benumbing the hands, and impeding all progress in the right direction."

It was the direct influence of this "dirt philosophy," Richardson believed, that led many people in the movement to deny any significant present-day role to the Holy Spirit and thereby foster a doctrinal formalism. In reacting against the abuses of the doctrine of the Spirit in popular theology, many leaders, he believed, had become "so extremely cautious upon the subject that, so far from cultivating religious feeling, they seem rather to repress it, and to encase religion within the ices of a philosophical sensibility."

Two extreme positions attracted many people, he thought. One he called the "Spirit alone" theory, the other the "Word alone" theory. On the one hand, the advocate of the "Spirit alone" view "imagines himself to have realized the presence of the Spirit in some emotional excitement, some brilliant vision, or some audible revelation." On the other hand, the advocate of the "Word alone" view "amuses himself with the notion that he has resolved all the mysteries of the Holy Spirit, when he has persuaded himself that this Spirit is merely a visible and tangible New Testament."

Both extremes, he said, pervert scripture's plain teaching about the work of the Spirit. But if forced to choose between the two views, he said, he would certainly choose the "Spirit alone" position, for such views "at least lead the mind to seek after fellowship with God; and embody the idea . . . that there is a real communion to be enjoyed with the spiritual world."

Richardson recognized that some people went to emotional excess in their religion, but he felt that the opposite extreme—a Spiritless faith—was an even greater evil. And so he steadfastly opposed those, including his close friend Alexander Campbell, who tended to reduce the Spirit's influence to the Bible alone. Campbell had insisted, for example, that since the Bible already "contains all the arguments which can be offered to reconcile man to God, and to purify them who are reconciled," therefore "all the power of the Holy Spirit which can operate on the human mind is spent."

Such views, Richardson believed, retarded spiritual vitality and growth. How many professed reformers there are, he exclaimed, "to whom the gospel has come 'in word only,' and who seem unable to make their way out of the cocoon of formalism, which enwraps them and their religion in perpetual immaturity!" Limiting the Spirit's influence to the Bible alone, he thought, "degrades the Bible, by placing it in a false position, and ascribing to it exclusive power and attributes which it never claims for itself."

"The Simple Faith of Primitive Times"

Throughout his many writings Richardson called his fellow believers to a religion of the Spirit, to a faith empowered by the personal indwelling of the Holy Spirit. With Christian faith beset by worldliness, compromise, formalism, and bitter controversies, how, Richardson asked, will a vital Christian faith be restored to the world? He answered: "by returning to the primitive faith and love; by doing the first works, and by a manifestation in the life of those fruits of the Spirit which alone reveal the truth of religion, and demonstrate to the world the divine mission of Jesus."

But in order to show forth the fruit of the Spirit, Richardson quickly added, "the presence of the Spirit Himself is necessary." Indeed, in the present day the presence of the Holy Spirit in a fuller measure is the "true want of the Church." People must "return to the simple faith of primitive times, and cease forever from those discords and dissensions which . . . have largely banished the Holy Spirit from the hearts" of professing Christians.

The Holy Spirit, Richardson said, is "God's missionary" to human hearts. The Spirit, he often affirmed, is "imparted to the believer, really and truly, taking up His abode in his person, as a distinct guest, or inhabitant." The Spirit is "God enthroned in man's moral nature, renewing and sanctifying the affections, and transforming humanity into the Divine image." The Spirit does this through "the graces it imparts and through the 'ingrafted Word' which it has introduced into the heart, and now ever preserves green in the memory and fruitful in the life."

Without the Spirit, Richardson thought, faith loses its true character, becoming more the adoption of a doctrinal system than of a spiritual life. Indeed, without the Spirit much that passes for orthodoxy is vain. "In vain do men weary themselves and the world with plans of reformation; with systems of belief; with schemes of union based on human wisdom. In vain do they imagine themselves to have discovered the secret of the power of the primitive church in its freedom from priestly rule; or in its super-natural gifts; or in any other exterior characteristic." The secret of the early church's power was nothing less than this: "the indwelling of the Spirit of God, giving unity, imparting energy, evolving the glorious fruits of Christianity, and presenting to the world, in every disciple, an illustration of the life of Christ."

"To Set the Heart Right First"

A most basic principle of the movement, Richardson said, was a distinction between "the Christian faith" and "doctrinal knowledge." What does it mean to believe in Christ? he asked. He answered that it means not simply to receive his doctrine or to believe what he says. Rather it means to be brought into "direct relation and fellowship with Him; to think of Him as a person whom we know, and to whom we are known." It means to speak to him and listen to him as one would to a close friend. "Christ is not a doctrine, but a person," Richardson urged.

At its heart Christian faith centers on a person, not a body of doctrines. It does not consist essentially in the "accuracy of intellectual conceptions," but rather in a certain kind of life—a transformed inner life and a fruitful outer life. People may possess "the same faith, while they differ greatly in the amount and accuracy of their religious knowledge."

The broad expanse of biblical doctrine, he carefully pointed out, must never be discounted, for it serves as an important superstructure. But it does not provide the foundation. That is found only in a deeply personal relationship with Christ—and "the foundation must precede the superstructure."

The main problem behind a fragmented Christian world, Richardson believed, is that people confuse trust in a living savior with belief in certain doctrines. When this happens faith gets "supplanted by polemics." Sectarian belligerence and rivalry mount. Doctrinal creeds, whether written or unwritten, become the basic measure of orthodoxy. And people inevitably grow distant from Christ. They grow distant, Richardson said, because a "syllabus of doctrine has no power to enlist the heart and the energies of the soul in the true work of Christ." Indeed, what "every true sectary lacks" is this personal reliance on Christ. He stands on the walls of his camp and asks those who seek to enter, not "In whom do you believe?" but rather "What do you believe?" He thinks that the error and confusion of the human heart will be remedied by intellectual opinions.

But his way is the way of human folly. The way of divine wisdom is "to correct the errors of reason by regulating the affections." "Oh! to set the heart right first," Richardson exclaimed, "saves the head a world of useless trouble, for it is truly through the heart alone that any one can comprehend the 'doctrine of God.'"

So "true religion," for Richardson, meant nothing else than entering into spiritual union with God. It meant contemplating the divine glory and the "ever-opening mysteries of redeeming love." It meant allowing oneself to be renovated into a living temple for the Holy Spirit.

"The Richest Service of All"

Throughout his life Richardson addressed these themes with a quiet passion and eloquence. In a time when doctrinal, polemical, and organizational matters preoccupied the movement, he remained a persistent—at times almost solitary—advocate of a deeper, richer spirituality. It was here, he felt, that the movement was most lacking. In 1842 he noted, for example, "a dull insensibility in respect to spiritual things, which seems to arise from an ignorance of there being any such thing as a true and spiritual union with God and Christ."

A few other voices had raised such concerns before him. John Rogers of Carlisle, Kentucky, for example, had written to Campbell in 1834, noting that "many of us, in running away from the extreme of enthusiasm, have, on the other hand, passed the temperate zone, and gone far into the frozen regions." "There is, in too many churches," he added, "a cold-hearted, lifeless formality, that freezes the energies." And Campbell himself, on a few occasions, could raise such concerns. Religion certainly was an intellectual matter, he wrote in 1837, "but religion dwelling in the heart, rooted in the feelings and affections, is a living, active, and real existence." This is what fills the soul with divine life. "This is religion," he concluded; "all the rest is machinery."

Richardson picked up such concern and made it a life-long focus. His writings resound with the call to the spiritual life. But nowhere is his vision of that life more powerful and eloquent than in his many communion meditations delivered to the Bethany church.

J. W. McGarvey was a student at Bethany College in 1847-48

and heard many of them. "The richest service of all," he later wrote, "was when they had a sermon by Mr. Campbell followed by Dr. Richardson in a five- or ten-minute talk at the Lord's table." These talks were gems of beauty, he said.

Between 1847 and 1850 Richardson published a series of the talks in the *Millennial Harbinger* under the title "Communings in the Sanctuary." Later, at the urging of McGarvey and others, he collected twenty-four of them into a small book of the same title. That book remains the first and greatest of the devotional books written in the movement.

At the heart of the book lies a constant sense of the awesome mystery of things human and things divine. Three themes predominate.

(1) *The mystery of the holy.* In Richardson's view, recognition of the divine mystery is fundamental to Christian faith. Far from hindering one's vision or obstructing one's spiritual progress, the recognition of mystery brings "truer and nobler" views of God. "In proportion as the mysteries presented to us deepen, they approach nearer to God," Richardson said. "He is the great mystery of mysteries, and we draw nearer to Him as we approach the veil that conceals his inner temple."

In pointing to the mysteries of faith, Richardson did not cast out reason. The Christian faith contains intellectual depths, to be sure, and the mind seeks to plumb them. Reason especially plays an important role in the "preliminary examination of the facts and evidences of the gospel." But reason's power is sharply limited. It simply cannot purify the heart and bring human passions under control. Only the gospel can do that. In purifying and transforming the heart the gospel reveals its greatest power and profoundest mysteries — here one finds that "a 'deeper deep' speedily exhausts the plumb line of reason and philosophy."

(2) *The mystery of Christ's atoning death.* Because Richardson prepared these talks for the communion service, they invariably cen-

tered in Christ's death. Though the coming of Christ into the world was a great mystery, he said, "how much greater the mystery of his death! What new and wonderful developments it gives of the divine character! What startling thoughts it suggests of things invisible!"

So inscrutable was the mystery of the atonement, many preachers in the movement thought, that dwelling on it or trying to explore it yielded little profit. One did better to affirm the simple historical facts, then turn to more practical and understandable matters—like what people must do to be saved.

Richardson thought otherwise. To him the events of Jesus' death were "transcendent facts" full of meaning and mystery. By fixing one's eyes there, troubled consciences and rough desires were stilled by the "potent charm of Jesus' love." By entering its dark places and exploring its deeps time and again one grew ever more captivated by holy things and higher loves. Indeed, in contemplating such mysteries, one came to "see more of God than angels knew before!"

3) *The mystery of union with God and Christ.* In Richardson's view the Christian faith was not "a mere system of salvation from sin," with the cross being one part of that system. Neither was Jesus' death simply a removal of sin's penalties. Its purpose rather was "to effect a renovation—a regeneration of the soul."

Many believers, he thought, view redemption as a kind of commodity "which they may obtain upon certain terms, of which the ministers of the Gospel are supposed to be the negotiators." But redemption is no negotiable commodity. Rather, it involves nothing less than a transforming union with God and Christ through the Holy Spirit.

This union is one of faith's great mysteries. Through it the believer develops entirely new spiritual sensibilities. As those senses are cultivated, the believer grows "as fully alive to the things of the spiritual world, as is the natural man to the things of the natural world." He develops "a fellowship with spiritual existences and objects of whose very existence he was formerly wholly unconscious." In a word, the believer becomes fit for life in heaven with God.

"Desperately Seeking Spirituality"

These meditations were reprinted early in the twentieth century but have long been out of print. They are being released in this new edition in the conviction that they will speak with freshness and power to contemporary Christians, especially Christians in the lineage of Barton Stone and Alexander Campbell.

The practice and theology of the Spiritual life has not been a central emphasis among the Stone-Campbell traditions. Yet it is to these concerns that more and more people, Christians and non-Christians alike, have turned in recent years. Spirituality, for good and for ill, has become the rage in a culture increasingly emptied and wearied by its own excesses. We have been treated to a plethora of popular prescriptions for the soul: Jungian therapist Thomas More's *Care of the Soul* and *Soul Mates;* endocrinologist Deepak Chopra's *The Seven Spiritual Laws of Success*; and astrologer James Redfield's *The Celestine Prophecy*, to name some of the more popular. The title of a 1994 *Psychology Today* article captured the mood: "Desperately Seeking Spirituality." Much of this literature is syncretistic, humanistic, and, measured by classical Christian standards, heretical. Many readers, no doubt, feel it has helped them in some way.

At the same time there has been among Christians a rediscovery of the rich and varied traditions of Christian Spirituality, ranging from the Desert Fathers, to Eastern Orthodoxy, to Pietism, to Wesleyan perfectionism, to twentieth-century pentecostalism. Popular writers like Richard Foster, Dallas Willard, Henry Blackaby, and Thomas Oden have mined this heritage in widely-read books. Books on the Spiritual life have proliferated, some of them theologically thin and faddish, but all of them together a sign of the spiritual seeking that marks this new time.

In view of this rediscovery, it is not surprising that perhaps the richest and most important theological work being done in our time

is on the doctrine of the Trinity. This foundational Christian doctrine, long in arrears in the modern age, is the necessary underpin-
ning of a balanced and dynamic Spirituality. It will enable Christians
to seek and experience a more intimate relationship with God, while
avoiding the extremes and fads to which our age is given.

Communings in the Sanctuary is a rich and well-balanced guide in
this regard. Dr. Richardson stood in the classical lineage of
Christian faith. His work is richly Trinitarian, a strong counter both
to an overly intellectualized faith and to an overly experiential one.
It will serve Christians well as we begin the third millennium.

Finally, I offer two cues for reading this book. One: This is a
work of devotion and should not be read like a novel, a collection of
inspirational essays, or even a work of theology. It should be read
slowly, with meditation and rereading, and in small portions. Just as
one would not wish to hear ten Lord's supper meditations in a row
at one Sunday assembly, so these meditations should not be heaped
together in one long period of reading.

Another cue: The syntax and cadence of the language are from
an earlier, less oral and more literate time. The conventions of language and sensibility were different, untouched by the powerfully
reshaping impact of electronic media. In editing this work, I have
altered the punctuation to bring it more into line with present stylis-
tic conventions; even so, the present-day reader may still have to
push through what seems at first to be syntactical impediments. But
there is an eloquence here and, more importantly, a Spiritual and
theological richness that more than repays the effort. And
Richardson's call to a deeper, fuller *experience* of the Divine life will
resonate in surprising ways with believers of a postmodern age who,
wearied and disillusioned with grand church schemes, find themselves simply wanting more of God.

Leonard Allen
March 2000

1

—

"How amiable are thy tabernacles, O Lord of Hosts!"

When the Patriarch arose from his dreamy slumbers in the field of Luz, he exclaimed, "Surely the Lord is in this place, and I knew it not!" How many thus enter into the sanctuary of God without any realizing sense of the divine presence! How many, alas, from that sleep of error never waken! Yet the Lord is in his holy temple and will there reveal himself to his people; even to the seed of Israel, his servant—the children of Jacob, his chosen.

How fitting that we should enter into his gates with thanksgiving and into his courts with praise. How proper that we should here repress each worldly thought and yield our hearts up to those sacred communings in which Faith lifts a ladder to the skies, that angels may descend to earth and God himself confirm his promises of grace. Surely with the lonely wanderer of Bethel, we may exclaim: How dreadful is this place! This is none other but the house of God, and this is the gate of heaven.

Here, indeed, we have no earthly holy place, framed and adorned by human hands; no inner temple veiled in mysterious sanctity; no golden emblems of the regalia of heaven; no Shechinah beaming forth from between the cherubims; but we have the assembly of the saints; the congregation of the Lord; the body of Christ animated by his Spirit; the ordinances of divine service revealing, publishing, commemorating the love of God to men; the holy privilege of drawing near to God in concert with those who have obtained like precious faith with us; the unveiled spiritual glories of the reign of heaven; the light of life; the joys of divine love. Return, then, unto thy rest, O my soul! for the Lord hath dealt bountifully with thee.

In the deep stillness of the heart let every anxious care be hushed and cheerful Hope diffuse her grateful balm. Let the sorrows of the mind be banished from this place, for the Being in whose presence we appear is the God of consolation and of hope. To him we bring no bleeding victim from the flock and present no ineffectual oblations upon a blazing altar, but we offer the incense of praise; the grateful homage of the affections; the deep devotion of the soul; the living sacrifice of the body, acceptable through the precious blood of the Lamb of God who takes away the sin of the world and emancipates us from the bondage of fear and sorrow.

With what heart-felt assurance, then, we should make his sheltering wings our refuge. With what reverential joy we should approach the sacred memorials of his grace here presented before us and "banquet on his love's repast." Behold these emblems. They speak to the heart. They tell of God's love—the love of Him from whom all love proceeds. They tell of sorrows borne for us—of humiliation, pain, and death. Let us consider them. We come to Jesus and he meets us here—

"The King himself draws near
To feast his saints today."

In the awful mysteries of life and death we hold communion. With the spiritual unseen we live and move. Into the dwelling of the Most High we enter to take the cup of salvation—to pay our vows in the presence of his people. May the words of my mouth and the meditations of my heart be acceptable in thy sight, O Lord, my Strength and my Redeemer.

2

―

"I was glad when they said unto me:
Let us go into the house of the Lord."
Psalm 122:1

It is indeed in the assembly of the saints that gladness and rejoicing should fill the heart. It is here that we are, in an especial manner, permitted to draw near to Him that is the source of every pure and blissful emotion. In his presence there can be no sorrow, for there all tears are wiped away and there are "pleasures forevermore." In the contemplation of his glory which also he permits us to enjoy; in the ever-opening mysteries of redeeming love; in the radiance of that divine illumination which penetrates the moral and intellectual powers, and reveals the past, the present, and the future, what unfailing sources of happiness are found.

And how delightful the reflection that this happiness can never end; that Infinity itself is our treasury of joy, in which are stored "the unsearchable riches of Christ"; that new discoveries await us which Fancy's bright imaginings but dimly sketch, and that these shall give place to hopes more radiant and a fruition still more glorious. It is thus that the unknown may forever continue to gratify our love of knowledge, and the untold mysteries of the universe augment that blissful experience which serves but to enlarge the capacity for enjoyment.

How strangely attractive indeed to us are the mysteries by which we are encompassed. How wisely arranged is our progress that new scenes continually open to our view and lead us onward to a better future. How appropriate here the reflections of Chateaubriand, that all "the beauty, sweetness, and grandeur of life reside in its mysteries; and that no condition can be more deplorable than that of a man who can learn no more! What delight continually fills the heart of youth which knows as yet so little! What satiety depresses the feelings of age to which life's changes have been all revealed! How fortunate for the latter, when the secrets of life are ending, those of eternity commence!

"The feelings of love and modesty, of friendship and gratitude, are involved in obscurity; yet how strongly do they move the heart! The angelic virtue of charity loves to withdraw itself from all regards, as though to conceal its celestial origin. The pleasures of thought, also, are in those sciences which always leave something to be discovered and fix our regards upon a perspective which is never to terminate.

"If, in the bustling city, we survey a modern monument, whose origin or purpose is known, it excites no attention; but, if we meet upon a desert shore a broken column or mutilated statue, worn by the lapse of ages, its pedestal covered with unknown characters, how interesting a subject of meditation it presents to the mind. Everything is concealed, everything is hidden in the universe. Man himself is the greatest mystery of the whole. Whence comes the spark which we call existence and in what obscurity is it to be extinguished? Our birth and death are placed by the Eternal, like two veiled phantoms, at the two extremities of our career. The one produces the inconceivable gift of life—mysterious amid its light; the other quenches that brilliant spark in the obscurity of its own impenetrable darkness."

It is not surprising that men should have availed themselves of the influence of mystery upon the human mind to impose upon it the chains of superstition. An affected sanctity, a claim of angelic visions, or of a miraculous power to heal secure at once the wonder and submission of the throng. The strange accents of the unknown language of the mass; the awful mystery of transubstantiation; the solemn ceremonies of a worship imperfectly understood: these are all calculated to take hold of the imagination and chain the soul.

Surely, however, it is not incongruous with the *real* mysteries of religion to throw around them those pleasing shades and grateful harmonies which so well display their nature and extend their power. The ancient tabernacle was shrouded in curtains; and, while the gorgeous temple shone in all the elegance of architecture, it had its deep recesses, its secret chambers, and its veiled mysterious sanctuary. Even the presence of the Deity was indicated by the *cloud* that filled these sacred abodes. For He who conceals himself in "light that no man can approach," "makes darkness his secret place—his pavilion round about him dark waters and thick clouds of the skies." And it is but a just conformity to the fitness of things, and an efficient aid to devotional feeling and the solemnity of public worship, to exclude at least the glaring brilliancy of day from the house of prayer. For, however well suited may be the dazzling beams of day to the town hall or the market where men transact the business of this world, the painful glare transmitted by uncurtained windows, revealing the naked walls, the rude benches, the rough table, and the clumsy rostrum sometimes met with in our houses of worship, seems illy to comport with the circumstances of the place and the solemnities of religion. Though we may indeed dispense with the "long-drawn aisle and fretted vault," the clustered pillars, the gorgeous tapestry, the carving and the gilding which merely gratify a love of worldly splendor, surely a decent respect for the service of the house of God should induce a careful attention to every means calculated to favor devotional feeling and sanctify those rites whose mysterious import claims the undivided attention of the soul.

How often may we justly impute to the absence of such aids that want of reverence which is so conspicious. How often are those wandering thoughts, those restless glances, those distracted feelings which are so readily marked, occasioned by those unpropitious arrangements by which the things and thoughts of the world are continually pressed upon the attention. In vain would heaven assist our faith by the sacred symbols of divine love and allure the heart to dwell upon spiritual joys, when the glare and bustle of everyday life are permitted to intrude themselves into the house of the worshiping assembly.

It is here that everything should promote that solemn stillness and that reverential awe which prepare the heart for communion with God and a better appreciation of the deep mysteries of his grace. It is in the contemplation of these that the soul reaches forward into an unseen eternity and anticipates the day when, freed from the trammels of mortality, it shall be free to explore those wonders now so imperfectly perceived and understood. It is in making new discoveries in the depths of divine wisdom and in gaining clearer insight into his unsearchable judgments that the Christian realizes the blissful privileges he enjoys.

Here, then, may the boldest fancy attempt its most adventurous flight, and the mind expand its noblest powers, and the pious heart experience its purest and holiest emotions. For there are no boundaries to the ocean of divine love. There are no limits to the riches of the divine wisdom. There are no fears that man shall ever find an end or weep that he can know and wonder and enjoy no more. "Praise thou the Lord, O my soul!" "Sing unto the Lord a new song and his praise in the congregation of the saints." "Praise God in his sanctuary, praise him in the firmament of his power! Praise him for his mighty acts; praise him according to his excellent greatness! Let every thing that hath breath praise the Lord!"

3

"I will abide in thy tabernacle forever:
I will trust in the cover of thy wings."
Psalm 61:4

How truly incomprehensible and beyond comparison is the love of God for man! Inscrutable as his ways, unsearchable as his judgments, deep as the exhaustless mines of his wisdom and knowledge, his love but partakes of the infinitude of his nature and the ineffable glory of his perfections. How, then, can we hope to fathom its depths, to estimate its value, or to realize its power? Were we to add together all the emotions of love in all human hearts; every feeling of affection; every sentiment of kindness; every form of attachment—parental, filial, fraternal, social, the love of the espoused, the love of lovers—all would fail to express or even typify the love of God. Of all these kind and affectionate emotions, these fountains of earth's joys without which this world would be a dreary waste, God is the author. For God is love in its abstract and unoriginated essence; and, since love can proceed from God alone, these are but the faint emanations, but the scattering rays of that divine love which first created and now redeems. And oh! how weak our noblest effort; how cold our warmest thought; how faint our most vivid conceptions when contrasted with this love.

Yet we are here assembled in presence of these sacred emblems to consider it in the most wonderful of all its manifestations. "In this was love, not that we loved God, but that he loved us and sent his Son to be the propitiation for our sins." Earth's highest evidence of love is that a man should die for his friends. To heaven belongs the love that brought Christ to die for his enemies. Earth can supply no comparison by which it may be illustrated and the human soul possesses no powers by which it may be fully appreciated.

He forsook those realms of joy where the love of God forever reigns; he abandoned the honors and wealth of heaven to assume our nature; to take the position of a servant; to become a pauper, an outcast, a homeless wanderer. He came to endure fatigue and hunger and temptation; to encounter contumely, ridicule, and scorn; to receive hatred for instruction and ingratitude for kindness; to be "despised and rejected of men"; to be emphatically "a man of sorrows" and one who was familiar with grief; and finally, in all his innocence and unresisting gentleness, to be made to suffer the ignominious death of the cross—reviled even in his agonies and not only by the cruel throng but by the faltering tongues of dying robbers, co-partners in shame and suffering; denounced by the vilest of men; and (oh, insupportable anguish) while thus cut off from life as unfit for earth, forsaken by the Deity as unfit for heaven.

Yet he suffered not for himself; he was not "stricken or smitten of God" or "afflicted" for his own offenses. For surely it was our griefs he bore; it was our sorrows that he carried. He was wounded for our transgressions; he was bruised for our iniquities. It was the chastisement of our peace that was upon him; it was by his stripes that we are healed.

Such are the wonderful facts which we are called upon to contemplate as the exemplification of the love of God. And certainly it is in the life and death of Jesus that we can best consider that love and make the closest approach to its apprehension. As Immanuel he has brought God near to us; as the express image of the Father he has truly revealed Him; as God manifested in the flesh, he is love impersonated. In all his acts we observe the power of this divine love; we study it in all his words; we recognize it in all the social intercourse, in all the familiar incidents of his life, and in all the affecting associations and fearful agonies of his death.

How proper that the Deity should desire this love to be reciprocated. Every emotion loves to reproduce itself and to find a kindred sympathy in the bosom of another. It is thus extended, exalted, and perfected in those of corresponding susceptibilities, and attains its legitimate objects. It is from man, who is created in the image of God, that God himself desires reciprocal love. And if poignant the sting of anguish experienced when earth's weak love is unrequited, what must be the keenness of the sense of ingratitude when the love of heaven is rejected with disdain—A love of whose intensity we can form no adequate conception—A love that pervades the universe; that includes all within its fond embrace and longs to impart its own ineffable joys to all who will receive them. Oh! may not even the angelic nature here feel a sympathetic pang?

May not the Son of God here shed bitter tears of anguish, as first on Olivet?

But, alas! how shall man return a love of which he can not even adequately conceive? It is high as heaven; it is vast as the universe. How can he attain to it? how can he compass it? Poor, indeed, must be his offering of a heart debased by the world and Satan, when all its purest and noblest feelings of undivided affection would bear no proportion to the love of God. But it is the nature of love never to be mercenary. It seeks not compensation, it requires not equal measure, it demands not more than can be given. A gentle word may requite a kind act; a smile of affection, the most precious favor. Man may not love as God loves, who is infinite in love as in wisdom and in power; but he may love as man can love, who is so limited and feeble in all his capacities. And when he loves the Lord with all his heart and mind and soul and strength, he renders the least return that may be offered and the greatest that can be demanded.

Nor is man left to form, by imagination, faint images of the Deity on whom his affections are to rest. Jesus is the living image of the invisible God and his manifestation in the flesh renders possible that personality of attachment, that individualization of love so apposite and congenial to our nature. Nay, we are not even left alone with the sweet remembrances of the personal advent of the Lord Messiah, gleaned from sacred and ancient records; but as though to give scope and expression to this love, and quicken it by the active energies of life, he supplies a present, living, coequal, and consentient object, and bids us prove our regard for him by our love for one another. "A new commandment I give unto you, That you love one another: as I have loved you, that ye also love one another."

"He that hath my commandments and keepeth them, he it is that loveth me: and he that loveth me shall be loved of my Father, and we will come unto him and make our abode with him."

Transcendent thought, that man can become a temple for the Deity. That the glorious Being, of whom our unequal powers can form no adequate conception and whose glory fills both earth and heaven, can yet find a dwelling place in the human heart. Inscrutable and sublime mystery that "he that dwelleth in love dwelleth in God, and God in him." "Yet hereby do we know that we dwell in him and he in us, because he hath given us of his Spirit." And oh! how joyful the reflection that however weak our powers, however imperfect our efforts, the Divine Comforter can shed abroad the love of God in our hearts, enlarge our capacities, transform all our feeble nature, render us partakers of the divine fullness and sharers in the everlasting joys and effulgent glory of the divine presence.

4

"Thou, which hast showed me great and sore troubles,
shall quicken me again, and shalt bring me up again
from the depths of the earth."
Psalm 71:20

It appears at first view somewhat strange that Christianity, which brings life and immortality to light and opens to Faith the transcendent glories of the spiritual world, should, nevertheless, have here assembled its votaries to present to their contemplation the emblems of death and sorrow. It would seem as though its far-seeing gaze were suddenly obstructed and its distant hopes obscured; or that all its movements and influences were reversed and its noblest purposes altered; so that now its paths, like those of earthly glory, "lead but to the grave." Nor is it a less singular thought that death should become, under any circumstances, a subject of commemoration: strange that the very consummation of human woes and the chief object of human fears could be made a matter of voluntary contemplation—a matter to be celebrated, a source of happiness and hope; and, stranger still, that we should have met to celebrate the death, not of an enemy, but of our best and truest friend.

But it is in the sanctuary of God that the enigmas both of life and death are solved; that the mysteries of religion and of humanity are revealed. It is here that truths concentrate; that extremes meet and the first and the last, the beginning and the end, are one. It is here that He who, in the beginning, brought light out of darkness, educes good from evil, joy from sorrow, life from death, and glory from dishonor. It is here that we begin truly to realize that we dwell amid the antagonisms of natural and spiritual contrarieties, and that an omnipotent and omniscient Friend has wisely ordained our lot, that we might become acquainted with opposite and contrary affections, and learn by experience how immeasurable the height of that supreme love which holds the nice balance of our destiny, and how unfathomable the depths of that divine wisdom which, from the very lowest abyss of misery and depression, builds up the loftiest abode of joy.

"Except you eat the flesh and drink the blood of the Son of Man," says Jesus, "you have no life in yourselves." This is but the expression of the law of our spiritual being. "This is the record, that the Father has given to us eternal life, and this life is in his Son. He that hath the Son hath life, and he that hath not the Son of God hath not life." If Jesus had not died we could not have lived; for it is only through him who died for us that we can live to God. It is only by partaking of that bread which came down from heaven and which was given for the life of the world that we can live forever.

How precious the life which this spiritual food imparts. How just and striking the relation between this life and the food by which it is sustained. As the life must correspond with that by which it is maintained, celestial life can be nourished only by the bread of heaven. Food that is itself corruptible can maintain only a perishable life. "Therefore," said our Lord, "labor not for the meat that perisheth." "Our fathers did eat manna in the desert," replied the Jews, "as it is written, He gave them bread from heaven to eat." "No," replied Jesus, "I say to you, Moses gave you not that bread from heaven." That manna was corruptible, for if kept it bred worms and perished; it could sustain, therefore, but a perishable life. It was evanescent and disappeared before the rising sun; it was fitted, therefore, only to support a life which, like a "vapor, appeareth but for a little time and then vanishes away." "Your fathers," he therefore added, "did eat manna in the desert and are dead."

But the food by which spiritual life is sustained is imperishable. "I am that bread of life," said the Redeemer. "That is the bread which cometh down from heaven, that a man may eat thereof and not die. I am the living bread which came down from heaven. If any man eat of this bread he shall live forever, and the bread that I will give is my flesh, which I will give for the life of the world." Thus it is "living," incorruptible food alone that can impart life and incorruptibility. And oh! how striking the literal fact which perfects the agreement of these truths, that when our Lord gave his flesh for the life of the world that "living food" saw no corruption. For he was the "true bread from heaven"; the celestial manna; the "bread of God which came from heaven to give life to the world." It was not possible that he should be held by death in the bondage of the grave. God would not leave his soul in Hades nor suffer his Holy One to see corruption. The food of spiritual life must be imperishable as that life, and a just correspondance must obtain between the figurative and the real; the type and the anti-type; the fact and the doctrine which the fact reveals.

How important, then, the solemn declaration: "Except ye eat the flesh of the Son of Man, and drink his blood, ye have no life in yourselves." How important to realize that there is this necessary connection between life and its food, and that as mortality and corruption depend upon food that is itself perishable, so eternal life is equally dependent upon that food which endures forever. Well, therefore, did our Savior say: "Whoso eateth my flesh and drinketh my blood hath eternal life, and I will raise him up at the last day. For my flesh is meat indeed, and my blood is drink indeed; He that eateth my flesh and drinketh my blood dwelleth in me and I in him."

How happy he who can truly realize by experience these precious spiritual truths. How blissful the assurance that, in becoming partakers of Christ, we share that divine nature in which life is inherent. How wonderful the thought that we who are but, as it were, the creatures of yesterday may lay hold of the very attribute of the Deity and be invested with imperishable life and joy. And how inscrutable the wisdom, power, and goodness which can thus cause the natural to give place to the spiritual; which can compel weakness to reveal power, and death itself to yield us life.

5

"He that dwelleth in the secret place of the Most High,
shall abide under the shadow of the Almighty."
Psalm 91:1

There is a religion of the imagination, as there is a religion
of the intellect or of the heart; for God may be an object
of fancy as well as of reason or of love. Alas! how many are
the gifted souls who dream away the trial-time of life in vain
illusions, unawakened to the realities of true devotion. And
how earnestly they seek to prolong those visions of ideal
beauty and dwell within those palaces of enchantment which
have arisen at their pleasure.

To them this universe is but as a fairy mansion whose
cerulean dome is studded with sparkling gems and sustained
by mountain columns whose capitals are brilliant glaciers of
magnificent proportions and carved with more than
Corinthian elegance. To them the sun shines forth through the

stained windows of the east only to sparkle in the dew-drops or to paint the flowers or to relieve with light and shade the imagery of earth and heaven; and he sinks into the golden aerial seas of the west amid clustered islands, glowing with the tints of the ruby and the amethyst, the fancied residence of perpetual delight. The orbs of the firmament are, to them, the lamps which night suspends from the lofty vault to cast a silvery radiance over field and stream and forest, and increase enjoyment by the charms of variety and the mysterious wonders of her still and shadowy hours. The whole earth, indeed, to them, is but a magnificent suite of apartments carpeted with verdure or paved with marble and embellished with living pictures.

In the vast halls and spacious courts of their abode the ear is soothed with the melody of birds and the senses lulled by the murmur of gushing fountains and the sweet odor of flowers borne on the wings of gentle zephyrs. In its secret cabinets are treasures inexhaustible of gold and silver and precious stones. Its pleasure grounds, its gardens, its groves, its river and lakes and oceans, filled with the various tribes of animated nature, are created to be admired and are but varied orders and forms of beauty. In a word, the world with all that it contains is, to them, but an exhibition of glory and beauty—an emanation from the Beautiful which is their deity and their idol. To this alone they offer the incense of their hearts; to this alone they build their altars, not only in the fair field of Nature but in the temples of Art. The sculptor, the painter, the musician, the architect, the poet, and the orator are the true priests of their religion; praise is their only oblation and pleasure their sole pursuit.

How generally are these the dreams of youth. How often

too are they the only realities of manhood. How many there are who live merely to cull earth's fading flowers. How many there are who worship at no other shrine than that of an ideal perfection of beauty—a sensual image—a worldly sanctuary—an earthly Zion, out of which the true Jehovah has never shone. With them a refined taste is the true standard of piety and an admiration of the works of the Creator true devotion.

Nor is their discernment of moral beauty less acute or accurate than their perception of the charms of Nature. They contemplate with delight its noble examples; they honor and admire magnanimity and courage, patience and fortitude, benevolence and mercy, and all the moral virtues; but unfortunately, as they commit the error of thinking piety to consist in a proper reverence for the beautiful in the works of God, so they imagine that, in morals, to honor virtue is to possess it and that to admire morality is to practice it.

A thousands charms, however, cluster around this religion of the fancy, as compared with the barren and undecorated religion of the intellect. Here calm Philosophy seeks to analyze the organisms of the spiritual system, or prying Curiosity would dissect those outward forms from which all life and beauty have departed. Here, minute distinctions, remote discoveries, ingenious speculations are the grand essentials of both piety and morals. And, while the religion of the fancy would revel in the sunlight which imparts its splendors to earth and delight to range amid the charms of a terrestrial home, the religion of the intellect would soar aloft to seek the source of day and, in the vain attempt to gain superior knowledge, become lost beyond earth's limits in outer darkness and perpetual winter.

It is this religion which inspires that spiritual pride which dogmatizes in matters of opinion and that intolerant bigotry which persecutes in matters of faith. It is this religion which infuses into men the lust of power and coolly calculates the profits of oppression. Before its tribunal the rights of conscience are invalid and the pleadings of the heart are disregarded, for its laws are the speculations of opinionism and the decisions of its judges are the cold abstractions of a perverted reason. In a word, under its domination to think right is to do right and to worship reason is to worship God.

But oh! that "Lamb as it had been slain"—that form that was "marred"—that loving heart that was "pierced"—these sacred memorials of that divine love now spread before us. Surely it is not here that such religions as these can triumph. It is not in the sanctuary of God that we shall either bow in the chambers of imagery or yield to the idolatry of reason. How poor and weak and valueless do they appear when the heart feels the love of God and the soul rejoices in the Beloved. How evanescent now the glories with which Fancy may deck her day-dreams. How visionary and false here are Reason's partial revelations of the Infinite. "It is Christ that died; yea, rather that hath risen again." "It is God that justifieth; who is he that condemneth?" "It is the Spirit that quickeneth; the flesh profiteth nothing."

Before the cross of Jesus the magnificence of earth is vanity and the power of intellect but pride. And oh! how much have they to unlearn, who have been taught in these schools of error, before they can realize that God's grace is glory, that his foolishness is wiser than men, and his weakness, superior strength.

But oh! my soul, rejoice in the Lord and be joyful in the

God of my salvation! The Lord is "a sun and shield," a strong tower of defense to them that trust him. He crowneth thee "with mercy and loving kindness," and satisfieth thee "with good things." He leadeth thee by the "still waters" in the "green pastures" where he feeds his flock. "He guideth thee in the paths of righteousness for his name's sake." How happy they who are permitted to dwell in the courts of the Lord and to behold his beauty as he appears in the sanctuary. Here shines forever the true lamp of wisdom; here is continually provided the bread of life; here ascends the most acceptable incense; and, behind the veil of outward symbols, we are admitted to bow before the spiritual mercy-seat, overshadowed by the wings of cherubim and the radiant glory of the divine presence. For this is the house of God, the "greater and more perfect tabernacle" which the Lord himself has erected for his own abode. It is here he would receive the grateful homage of the heart. It is here that he will meet with those who love him and hope in his mercy.

And it is here that the deceitful visions of Fancy must be exchanged for the sacred promises of Christian Hope and that Reason must be subjected to the mysteries of Revelation. And oh! how gainful is that exchange! how blissful that subjection! For Christian Hope admits to scenes more glorious than unaided Fancy ever sketched and the mysteries of Faith are more sublime than those of Reason. And it is in the unsearchable riches of Christ, in the infinitude of the Divine perfections, the depths of his wisdom, the greatness of his power, the wonders of his redeeming love, that all the faculties of our nature may find their noblest exercise and most illimitable freedom. Here Fancy may range in fields of delight or rest in bowers of Eden, for Hope and Joy shall lead her to the realms of eternal glory where the perfection of beauty shall be enjoyed forever. Here Reason may be borne on wings of Faith to know and to admire the mysteries of the universe, while unfailing Love, enthroning the Deity in the heart, consecrates every pursuit, sanctifies every emotion, refines every enjoyment, and brings the whole man, in all the departments of his nature, under the blissful influences of true religion.

6

"I will come into thy house in the multitude of thy mercy,
and, in they fear, will I worship toward thy holy temple."
Psalm 5:7

The subjects to which our attention is here invited are of
the highest importance. Religion does not occupy herself
with trifles or present to our consideration the light matters of
a passing hour or of a fleeting fancy. Ah! no. Her themes are
serious and they are urged upon us with a solemn earnestness
appropriate to their character. We come not to the house of
God to gaze upon a display of beauty or of finery, to listen to
the voice of earthly pleasure, or dwell upon the idle vanities of
the world. Far different objects meet here the eye of faith, far
different is the voice that here salutes the listening ear, far different are the themes that here engross the soul. It is with life
and with death we come to hold communion and, amid the
solemn darkness and awful secrets of the grave, to find the
light and the revelations of eternity. Surely, that which thus

regards the deepest interests must be itself important; that which thus deals alone with realities must itself be real; that which allies itself equally to the dreary desolations of the grave—our mortal fears, and to our eternal hopes—the smiling joys of life and light and love, must claim our earnest and sincere regard.

How serious should be our thoughts of life! how solemn our meditations upon the mysteries of our being! how impressive our consciousness that we are raised up from the dust to move amid "this breathing world," to wrestle with its giant forms of evil, to struggle with the ever-watchful destroyer, and to contend for life even unto death! How abiding should be the conviction that we are inhabitants of two worlds and partakers of two natures—associated as well with the lowest form of animal existence as with the loftiest development of spiritual being; that there are ties which bind us both to earth and heaven, the seen and the unseen, the temporal and the eternal. How earnest should be our efforts to maintain our relations with life, and especially with that "eternal life which was with the Father" and was "manifested" to the world.

Who can contemplate, unmoved, the dissolution of this mortal nature; the cessation of the life-pulse that sends the vital current through the frame; the breaking up of those conscious springs of existence which we feel within us? How solemn and how sad those moments when we approach the last hour of life, even though our pains may be soothed by the kind hand of affection and our hearts comforted by the tender voice of sympathy, or consoled by the sweet assurances of forgiveness and sustained by the cheering promises of hope.

How dreadful, then, must have been the death which we now commemorate—the death of our Redeemer. Those who had attended him in life "stood afar off" and the sins of a world oppressed him with deadly anguish. By the mouth of the Prophet he exclaims: "Reproach hath broken my heart, and I am full of heaviness; and I looked for some one to take pity, but there were none; and for comforters, but I found none. They gave me also gall for my meat, and, in my thirst, they gave me vinegar to drink." "I am poured out like water, and all my bones are sundered. My strength is dried up like a pot-sherd, and my tongue cleaveth to my jaws, and thou hast brought me into the dust of death. For dogs have encompassed me; the assembly of the wicked have enclosed me; they pierced my hands and my feet. I may tell all my bones; they look and stare upon me. They part my garments among them, and cast lots upon my vesture."

The crucifixion of Christ was the greatest crime ever committed by men. He died by sin as well as for sin. Well did he say that "the blood of all the prophets which was shed from the foundation of the world should be required of that generation," for his death was the consummation of all their crimes. It is, indeed, often hard to realize that human beings could be guilty of so cruel an enormity; that they could so harm the harmless and pursue with such cruel animosity that good and gentle One. It seems so contrary to the common occurrences of life and to the common sympathies of humanity, which will be awakened in behalf of even the most atrocious criminal who is led along to execution, that we pause for a moment, in astonishment and wonder, to inquire, How can these things be? But again, when we reflect upon the power of Satan to inspire the human heart with his own malignity; when we remember what reason he had to seek the destruction of Jesus, who had resisted all his temptations, invaded his own dominions, and dispossessed his legionary tormentors of their prey, we can comprehend the fact and explain the enigma. And when we refer to the persecutions of the martyrs and to the inconceivable malignity evinced against the true followers of Jesus on his account, we see but the agency of the same mighty power of darkness and of death.

With how much bitter animosity and hatred has he inspired even the unbeliever who, from his own principles, should have been but an indifferent spectator of religious controversies and sectarian crimes. "Let us crush the wretch!" exclaims Voltaire, the prince of infidels; and have not his followers in our day been known with dying lips to curse the name of Jesus? Here we have, so to speak, our own experience to corroborate that wondrous tale of sorrow related by the evangelists, to show that it is possible for men thus to hate with such deadly and bitter hatred one who never harmed them but who, on the contrary, bestowed upon them the most precious favors. Yes, they hate him now as they hated him then, "without a cause." They would even now "crush" or crucify him and still vainly be called upon to answer the inquiry which Pilate propounded to his murderers: "Why, what evil hath he done?"

Who can approach, without trembling, to look in upon a soul thus filled with malignity? Who can, without a shudder, gaze into that dark abyss of wickedness into which human nature may thus be plunged? Who can duly estimate the capacities of men for crime when the dark Spirit of Evil himself undertakes to develop them? Yet such are the scenes we are called upon to witness, such are the subjects we are here invited to consider, where Christ crucified is placed before us and the scenes of Calvary are brought to our remembrance.

From this position we may survey that cruel spectacle and hear the mockery and the shouts of the infuriated crowd. They offer to him that narcotic bitter, in sour wine, which the Romans, to add the semblance of mercy to cruelty, were wont to give the condemned before their crucifixion to deaden their sensibility to pain; but when he tastes thereof he will not drink it. No. It is the cup which the Father hath given him that he will drink. It is the punishment due to our sins that he will endure without mitigation or alleviation. Behold him in those mortal agonies, and hear even his fellow-sufferers revile him, and see the disciples whom he had so fondly loved and so highly honored forsake him in the hour of his calamity.

But hearken to that sole complaint which he can be made to utter: "My God, my God, why hast Thou forsaken me?" The mortal pangs of expiring nature he can bear without a murmur and endure that he should be abandoned by his friends, but not that God should also forsake him. He can suffer the death of the body with unshrinking fortitude, but not that his soul should be separated from God, the source of being and of blessedness. Who can depict the expression of agony which rests upon that gentle countenance when he is thus excluded from both worlds and left, for one dreadful moment, alone with human crimes? Upon that pure and innocent nature how heavily presses that sinful load! Before his sacred soul appear in horrid array the unnumbered transgressions of the whole world, from that of Eden—the murder of Abel—the crimes of Manasseh—the blood of Zechariah—the cruelty of his own destroyers—the persecutions of his martyrs—the revolting detail of all the forms of human guilt now known or yet to be. And are not our sins, too, there, while cruel lips mock that cry of agony and say: Let us see if Elijah will come to save him? and while cruel hands present him vinegar to drink?

Surely, he was wounded for our transgressions; he was bruised for our iniquities; the chastisement of our peace was upon him, and with his stripes we are healed. For it pleased the Lord to bruise him, to put him to grief, to make his soul an offering for sin, and he has laid on him the iniquities of us all.

For this "he hath trodden the wine-press alone, and of the people there was none with him." For this he is "despised and rejected of men." For this "he is taken away by distress and judgment" and "cut off out of the land of the living" in the morning of life. Who now shall give an account of his race? "Who shall declare his generation?" What name or memorial has he left in Israel? Is there not one to mourn for him? not one to bear his name to future ages? Yes, says the Spirit, it is even now, when his soul is made an offering for sin, that "he shall see his seed," that he "shall prolong his days," and that "the pleasure of the Lord shall prosper in his hand." "He shall see of the travail of his soul and be satisfied." He shall rejoice in a numerous posterity that God shall give him—the children of faith and love, the children of the resurrection, of light and life. For "I will divide him a portion with the great, and he shall divide the spoil with the strong, because he hath poured out his soul unto death, and was numbered with transgressors, and bore the sin of many, and made intercession for the transgressors."

Through this offering God can be just in justifying the ungodly. Through his death God has brought to light incorruptibility and life, and the greatest crime ever committed by man has been made to us the richest blessing. It was Satan's doing to instigate men to slay him; it was the Lord's doing to destroy, through his death, him that had the power of death and to deliver human souls from bondage. Let the earth rejoice and break forth into singing, for the grave shall not devour forever nor continue to rob us of our joys. Death itself is made to bring forth life and the tomb becomes the chrysalis of immortality.

And shall not we, then, who have known the love of God approach with reverence this sublime mystery, to these emblems of death—of that death that gives life, the death of Jesus? Shall we, like his trembling attendants, stand afar off from Calvary? Shall we not rather, through the mocking crowd or through the thick darkness that shrouds the earth, approach the cross that we may behold the Lamb of God that takes away the sins of the world? Shall we not draw near to him that we may be sprinkled with his blood that speaks better things than that of Abel? and that we too may ask, like his penitent fellow-sufferer, to be remembered when he comes to his kingdom?

7

"I will ransom them from the power of the grave;
I will redeem them from death:
O death, I will be thy plagues;
O grave, I will be thy destruction."
Hosea 13:14

The universe consists of the living and the lifeless. The life-less exists by the living, since all things proceeded origi-nally from the creating power of God. The lifeless exists also, not only by the living, but for it--for the glory of him who cre-ated it--for the use of the living which he has created.

The lifeless can impart no life, since it does not possess it. Everywhere in nature it is the living that imparts life. In vain would we attempt to produce the humblest plant without the seed which incises within its woody husk the mystery of life. That seed has transmitted from age to age the animated germ formed by the first plant that grew. It is that living archetype alone which has power to appropriate to itself the unorganized elements of material nature and to evolve the living organization to its just proportions. Yet it is the lifeless which is made on earth the basis and the sustenance of the living. The animal may have fed upon the plant, but the plant has derived its sustenance from the lifeless materials of the inorganic world and yields, in its own death, those elements to the living.

It is in religion as in nature, not only that the living proceed alone from the living, but that life is sustained by death. The seed that germinates is the word of God that lives and abides forever. It is the Spirit that quickens. "As the living Father hath sent me," said Jesus, "and I live by the Father, so he that eateth me, even he shall live by me." Yet this "bread of heaven" is he that died that he might give life—this living food is the flesh and blood of a crucified Redeemer.

It is here, then, in view of these sacred emblems of the divine philanthropy that we may appreciate that strange and solemn truth, as fully verified in respect to the body as the soul, that we can live by death alone. Not only do we sustain our animal life by the lifeless forms of once living plants and animals, but even our own corporeal frame itself subsists by its own decay and, like the light of a lamp, lives by the very waste that tends to destroy it. How well we know, then, that we can live only by that which has died for us—by that which has yielded its life for ours. And how admirably the irrevocable arrangements of Nature itself illustrate the no less immutable laws of divine grace.

How like the work of God that Death should bring forth Life. It was he who created the world out of nothing, who brought light out of darkness. How appropriate that he should bring life out of death. This was the work of God. This was the mission of Jesus. He came to abolish death; to destroy, through death, him that had the power of death and to bring life and incorruptibility to light. How glorious the triumph when the enemy is not merely conquered, but compelled to act as a friend until the hour of his destruction. How inconceivable the power, wisdom, and goodness which can thus reverse extremes and reconcile opposites, educing salvation from ruin, life from death, and incorruptibility from the grave.

Jesus died. He belonged to both the lifeless and the living; and of these great classes must all be members. The living shall become lifeless; again, the lifeless shall become the living. It is the struggle of Life to conquer Death, and this was the combat and the victory of Jesus; and this, too, is the contest and, through him, the triumph of his people. As the germ, touched by the life-giving light of heaven, struggles through the darkness of the clod and lifts itself aloft toward the skies, so the awakened soul springs up to meet and enjoy the vivifying influences of the Sun of Righteousness. How joyful are his beams! how grateful his invigorating power! how glorious his light of life! How ennobling to contend thus against death and thus with Jesus to wage a warfare against the powers of darkness. How noble the enterprise which the Christian shall thus achieve, and how vain the triumphs of earth's proudest conquerors when compared with the victory of Life over Death—the rescue of the ransomed from the grave.

Earth's conquerors have fought to live upon the scroll of earthly fame. That moth-eaten scroll contains their names alone. They triumphed by means of death and pyramids of skulls have been their appropriate monuments; or the cold and lifeless marble, crumbling beneath the touch of Time, and vainly endeavoring to record, by a defaced intaglio, their works of slaughter. Their monuments but record that they have perished and these monuments shall perish with them. But the monument by which Jesus is here remembered commemorates the destruction of Death's power, the victory of Life, the conquest of eternal joy and renown. This monument is not a proud mausoleum, a stately obelisk, a sculptured pillar. This loaf, this cup of blessing, these appropriate elements—lifeless but life-sustaining—speak of Him who became lifeless that we might live by Him.

It is in these that faith beholds that celestial manna, that living food, that bread of heaven, which gives life to the world and sustains the soul amid the conflict against the powers of death. And these sacred emblems shall continue to publish in every land and amid all the nations and tribes of earth the dying love and life-giving power of Jesus until death itself is swallowed up in victory.

8

"We have thought of thy loving kindness, O God!
in the midst of thy temple."
Psalm 48:9.

How charming is the natural scenery around us. How beautiful the lofty hills which enclose this fertile valley like a gigantic circumvallation. How picturesque their varied forms; here, with gently sloping sides and rich pastures reaching to their summits; and there, precipitous and rock-ribbed, crowned with native forests. How pure and bright the blue heavens above. How grateful the soft verdure of the earth beneath. How great the joy of existence. How dear those vital sensibilities which connect us with these objects.

But here shall dubious and desponding thought point to those tombs and say: "This world would, indeed, be beautiful if there were no graves." And, truly, time was there were none. Time was when God himself looked abroad upon the land and sea and all that they contain, upon the verdant earth and the blue heavens, and blessed them in their beauty. How glorious then their charms! How abundant and undefiled their joys! No sorrow nor sighing then rent the suffering breast, nor pain nor anguish agonized the frame, nor decay nor malady nor violence led trembling captives to grace the triumphs of Death. For Life then reigned supreme amid scenes of pure felicity, over realms uninvaded by a hostile foot and unvisited by fear of change. And there were then no graves.

But what has made these graves and erected these monuments of Death? What malignant Power has thus marred the beauty of the world and robbed it of its joys? Are not these the consequences of sin, the desolations of Death, the woes of mortality, the sad tokens of guilt and condemnation? O Sin! thou sting of Death! thou minister of woe! how great have been thy victories! how vast they conquered realms! how galling the tyranny of thy power! These are thy trophies—more widely spread than those of Grecian or of Roman conquerors. These are thy triumphs, unfettered by mountain chains and unlimited by ocean depths, whose memorials are in the dark caves of the deep waters and upon the high places of the earth.

Thine, indeed, O Death, is the only universal empire that has ever flourished. How vain the enterprises of an Alexander, the laurels of a Caesar, the victories of a Napoleon. It was by thee they conquered and by thee they were themselves subdued. They reigned over a few territories—over a few of the people of a single generation; but thou over all lands, all earth-born cities, and all generations of men.

Yet are these graves, indeed, so dread a memorial of departed joys? And would the world be happy and beautiful if there were no graves? Could we now banish Death and live forever amid these earthly scenes would this be felicity and eternal joy? Ah! no; never while sin remains! never while unrighteousness and the unrighteous dwell on earth! If the longevity of the antediluvian world contributed to create giants in wickedness and to fill the earth with crime and violence until one faithful individual alone remained, what would be the condition of human society if Death placed no barriers in the way of crime? How soon would the rank and hardy weeds of unrighteousness overgrow and choke the tender and delicate plants of godliness. The very qualities which characterize the righteous—the gentleness and meekness, the humility, resignation and love which belong to their very nature—cause them to shrink and perish beneath the rage of the fierce and reckless passions and the proud oppressions of the ungodly.

How happy is it, then, that Death in time suspends the conflict. Happy, that as the frost of winter consigns alike the delicate and the luxuriant herbage to the dust in order that in early spring the contest may be again renewed on equal terms, so Death leaves free to the coming generation the field of the world for the great controversy of good and evil. Oh! then, how great a friend to righteousness is Death while sin yet dwells on earth. How potent an ally to curb the pride of the haughty and to break in pieces the oppressor. What sorrows has he not soothed! What pains and agonies of life has he not assuaged! Of what deliverances has he not been the author! How indispensable have been his services!

Need we wonder that when other consequences of sin have been removed and sin itself destroyed, Death will yet remain—once the first among the powers that have ruled over man in his rebellion, and now the last to be dispensed with among those that have served in his restoration to the divine favor. For if Death reigned by sin, Jesus has reigned by Death and shall deliver up the kingdom to the Father as soon as Death shall be no more.

Shall we say then: It is Death that robs us of our joys. It is the grave that mars the beauty of the world. Surely it is not Death by which Christ triumphed. Surely it is not the grave in which Jesus once reposed. Ah! no. Death is now to us the gate of heavenly joy—these graves are now earth's glory, since that of Jesus is among them. Behold his tomb! No proud monument of earthly pride; no Egyptian pyramid; no spacious mausoleum to commemorate, not the dead who lie beneath—their very names unknown—but the power of death that conquered them; no lofty pillar reaching to the clouds and erected by human hands but a NATIVE ROCK—fit sepulcher for the Author of Nature—a grave whose deep recesses have brought forth life and incorruptibility, and which is a memorial, not of the dead, neither of Death, but of the living and of Life.

These tombs, then, shall no longer mar the beauty of the world around us, since that of Jesus makes them but emblems of the destruction of the grave and types of joy to come. Let us, then, approach their salutary shelter and dwell amid their shades. Let the sorrows of death become our joys, its mourning our rejoicing. Let tears be sweeter than laughter and prayer than merriment and penitence than pride and Christ than all the world and his cross and sepulcher than home with all its joys. For death is now the Christian's captive and the grave his legacy of life—the dawn of mortality's night—the spring of an endless year that knows no winter.

9

"Whom have I in heaven but thee?
and there is none upon the earth that I desire besides thee."
Psalm 73:25

How precious to the heart of the Christian the high privilege of fellowship with God. How poor, in comparison, are all the pleasures of sense and all the honors of the world. It is to meet with the King Eternal, Immortal and Invisible, amid the sacred mysteries of his spiritual temple, that we are here assembled. We come to seek from that holy presence those elevating and consoling influences which impart a divine peace to the soul and purify the affections from the polluting touch of life's vain idols. We come to approach the fountain of being and of blessedness, to drink of its ever-flowing streams of eternal life and joy.

How holy and how reverend is the name of God! How awful the deep mysteries of the Divine nature! That name, that nature, constitute the study of life. Even amid the darkness of heathenism men strove to grope their way to God, and the multitude of their idols, while it shows the failure, proclaims also the earnestness of their search. And how powerful the influence of the ideas which men entertain of God. How their conceptions of the divine character modify their own. How successful the effort of Satan to degrade man by perverting his views of God. And how purifying, elevating, ennobling the contemplation of that Divine Creator, as seen within the sanctuary in which his glory stands revealed.

It is here, amid the sublime visions beheld by the eye of Faith, that God addresses himself to mortals. It is here that his wondrous works are interpreted by precious words. It is here that he appears in his true character as the Great Lord and Creator of the universe, material and spiritual. How glorious the attributes assigned to him in the ancient scriptures, of infinite power, wisdom, goodness, justice, truth, and holiness. How endearing the characteristics which the New Testament still more clearly reveals, of love, mercy, and condescension. By these he approaches us most nearly; by these we realize that God is with us, our Emmanuel, and are emboldened to enter into that divine fellowship to which he here invites us.

If it be granted, as some imagine, to each class of sentient beings in the dominions of nature to perceive its own position and understand the classes that are below it, to man is conceded, with self-consciousness, the loftier privilege of understanding, not only the classes that are below, but those also that are above him. Placed, as it were, in the middle position of the universe and blending in himself the material and the spiritual, he can reach to the lowest ranks of being and also to the highest—even to God himself. He can contemplate every facet of life and every variety of nature. Collecting the traces of the divine presence in his works, he can connect them with the Being from whom they issue and, ascending upon the wings of Faith, hold sweet communion with the Infinite and Eternal One.

To establish and maintain this communion is the great end of religion. To unite the soul to God; to erect in the human heart a living temple for his abode; to secure the enjoyment of that Divine presence which is the earnest of eternal blessedness: these are its noble and exalted aims—its truest, holiest purposes. And oh! how intimate is that fellowship to which we are thus introduced by the true and living Word. With how much confidence, with how much earnestness we are permitted to address ourselves to God . Under how endearing a title we are invited into his presence. As sons to a compassionate father, we approach him to hear his words; to rejoice in his power, wisdom, and love; to cast our cares upon him and to repose in the faithful assurances of his unceasing favor. As heirs of God and co-heirs of Jesus, we are invited to rejoice in an undefiled, unfading, and eternal inheritance—in the glorious prospect of being admitted to behold the glory of God and of the Lamb, and to share with the redeemed the pure perennial bliss of heaven.

And oh! how precious are the influences of that spiritual fellowship which we are permitted to enjoy. How dear to the soul should be every opportunity of cultivating that sacred intimacy, that divine acquaintanceship. How greatly we should desire to draw more closely still the ties that attach us to the heavens. The heart that becomes familiar here with the things of futurity—the soul that is here wont to enjoy habitual intercourse with God will be no stranger when admitted to the skies. Oh! how sweet it is on earth to have a friend, familiar with our thoughts and feelings, to whom we can unbosom all our cares and all our joys. But what friend can know the soul as God can know it? To what kind ear can we so unreservedly communicate our wishes, anxieties, and hopes? And with what human spirit, encased in mortality, can we form an alliance, a union, a fellowship, so intimate and so complete as with that divine and gracious Being who, by his Spirit, dwells within the heart itself and, partaking in the deepest secrets of the soul, anticipates our thoughts, interprets all our wishes, and intercedes for all our wakening hopes? Surely the renewed soul, thus intimate with God on earth, will be no stranger when ushered into heaven. Surely it will be thus suitably prepared for the blissful fellowship of the brighter realms above.

It is the contemplation of infinite excellence that exalts, as it is the society of the good and the noble that inspires nobility of soul. Unable of ourselves, perhaps, to form high conceptions and without "the bold warmth that generously dares," we catch, by degrees, something of the soaring spirit of the virtue that belongs to the noble minds with which we enjoy habitual intercourse and thus learn to share and to imitate the excellencies we admire. It is thus that communion with Perfect Goodness shall lead us to be good. Infinite Holiness and Purity shall inspire us with pure and holy affections, and the love of God, awakening in the heart a kindred emotion, shall transform the soul and invest our nature with a divine beauty. It is while we contemplate the glory of the Lord in the brilliant mirror in which his perfections are revealed that we are "changed into the same image from glory to glory, as by the Spirit of the Lord."

10

"I will remember the works of the Lord;
surely I will remember thy wonders of old.
I will meditate, also, on all thy works, and talk of thy doings.
Thy way, O God, is in the sanctuary;
who is so great a God as our God?"
Psalm 77:11-13

The sanctuary of God is the house of Memory and of Hope. It is here that we are presented with the only true record of the distant past. It is here alone that the solemn events of the approaching future are revealed to us. It is here that the two sacred institutions which unite to commemorate the death and the resurrection of Jesus harmoniously blend also the extremes of human destiny and, reconciling grief with joy, unite the darkness of the grave with the light of life.

How sweet are the memories which are here awakened. How consoling the remembrances of the divine love which are here so eloquent of hope and peace. With how much happiness may the Christian look back upon the past, which aims not, like the retreating Parthian, a single shaft to wound him. With what feelings of adoration and love may he lift his eyes to that face so "marred" and gaze upon that divine form so wounded for his transgressions and bruised for his iniquities. How he may, in that contemplation, realize the mysterious enchantment which heals the dread malady of sin and transforms the soul anew. How stilled by the potent charm of Jesus' love are all the bitter reproaches of conscience. How soothed the trembling fears of retribution. How calmed the hopeless agonies of despair. How vainly may the soul seek for the record of its guilt upon the sands over which the rising tide of the divine philanthropy has flowed. How unsuccessfully may it strive to reaminate the sins that were crucified with Christ. It is Christ alone that rises from the tomb of Joseph. It is our Savior and not our guilt that comes to meet us here. It is the gentle voice of our Redeemer that cries to us, amid the memories of the past and from these memorials of his love, "weep not."

But, ah! how different is the condition of the dwellers in the world without. That world is the abode of fear and of remorse. No grateful memories there pour the balm of consolation into the heart torn with anguish. No anodyne of pardoning love there soothes the pangs of unavailing regret. No voice of mercy there speaks peace to the soul tossed upon the dark waters of carnality and crime. Neither does the dayspring of hope arise to dissipate the gloom or gild the threatening clouds of futurity. But Fear and Horror brood over the stormy chaos of unholy passions and there mold the hideous spectral forms which haunt the guilty conscience and goad the soul to madness. How dreadful is the condition of those who are "without hope and without God in the world." How dark and dreary and desolate their pathway through the waste howling wilderness of life, who have no promise of a "pleasant land" beyond the Jordan's swelling flood.

But oh! how sweet are the consolations which here gladden the present by the joyful assurances of the future. How bright, how cheering, and how life-giving are the beams of Hope which here dissipate the darkness of ignorance and reveal to us the wide horizon of human destiny. How lofty is that sacred Pisgah to which the angel of the divine covenant here leads us, that we may not only contemplate with delight the grateful streams, the fruitful plains, and the vineclad hills of our inheritance, but rest in the conviction that we shall be led under conduct of our Joshua to enjoy them. It is here that our Divine Leader marshals us beneath the banners of love. It is here that he guides our weary feet toward those heavenly shores. It is here, by the sacred ark of the divine faithfulness and truth and amid the certain assurances of a glorious triumph, that the voice of Jesus cries to us, "Fear not."

Oh! how often, while on earth, did Jesus pronounce those words of consolation and encouragement: "Weep not!" "Fear not!" But, ah! it was he himself who wept that we might rejoice; who feared that we might hope. It was he who suffered that we might enjoy, who died that we might live. And oh! transporting thought, it is he who also revives and reigns that we, too, may rise to behold and share his glory and rest forever in the blissful mansions which he has prepared for our abode. So that, while in these memorials of the past we see him as he was, it is there, in the glories of the future, that we shall see him as he is; and, while the remembrance of his atoning love imparts sweet consolation, the hope of an eternal reunion inspires the soul with courage and leads us forward to the fruition of an eternal blessedness.

11

———

"Open to me the gates of righteousness:
I will go into them, and I will praise the Lord."
Psalm 118:19

How complete is the atonement which the gospel of Christ reveals. The work of a perfect Being, and perfect like its Divine Author, it requires no addition; it endures no compromise with the officiousness of human vanity and pride; it admits of no improvement by the wisdom of the world. Like the sun in heaven—which is unapproachable, yet comes to us in light and life and joy; which imparts its blessings to the wide-spread earth but can receive therefrom no addition to its beams—the atonement accomplished by the Redeemer, while it shines forth in all the effulgence of the divine philanthropy for the salvation of man, remains alone in its completeness, and while it bestows its saving mercies, can receive no augmentation of its efficacy from human works of righteousness.

Yet ah! how unwilling is the human heart to acknowledge its entire dependence upon the divine mercy. How prone is the unenlightened mind to seek some means of participating in the divine work. How apt is human pride to whisper to the soul that its own efforts have gained, at least in part, its own redemption. For what are the cruel rites of heathenism to placate offended idols; what the penance and mortifications of Catholic superstition to atone for sins, or the presumptuous prayers of misguided enthusiasm, supposed to render God propitious to the sinner, but various forms and applications of the fundamental error that man is or can be more willing to be saved than God to save him; that he has something more to do than simply to accept forgiveness, and must perform some work in aid of the divine means of salvation? Alas! it is when grace superabounds on the part of Heaven that man is most wanting to himself. It is when the religion of love is freely offered for his acceptance that he prefers the self-imposed cruelties of an exacting superstition.

Man meddles with the divine arrangements but to mar them. His touch defiles what is clean, his ignorance impairs what is perfect, his perversity embitters and poisons every divine fountain of happiness. God bestowed life, but man has mingled it with death and made it mortal. The Creator made man upright, but man has corrupted himself by his inventions. Jehovah wrought wonders in the earth and gave his statutes to Israel, but his people "forgot his works, and waited not for his counsel, but lusted exceedingly in the wilderness and tempted God in the desert, until he gave them their request, and sent leanness into their soul."

But God is "the Rock; his work is perfect, for all his ways are judgment; a God of truth and without iniquity, just and right is he." And oh! what infinite goodness appears in all his dealings with men, whether in nature or religion. How has he ever connected enjoyment with the use of the means required for life and rendered even pain tributary to pleasure. How sweet it is to breathe the balmy air around us. How grateful the exercise of a function so indispensable to existence. How delightful to him that is hungry the food by which he is sustained. How pleasant to him that is thirsty the cool waters of the fountain. Everywhere in nature man finds supplied to him the means of pleasure in the means of life, and is led by desire to fulfill the conditions of his being. He can create nothing, he can impart no quality of excellence, he can improve no divine method. He can but receive, accept, enjoy what God has formed and perfected for his use.

And is it not also in religion that man can only accept the divine mercies, and that he shall be led to their acceptance by an awakened desire for that spiritual blessedness which they impart? Can human reason improve upon the divine plan of salvation or man's feeble powers add efficacy to the means of spiritual renovation which God has instituted?

What can be conceived superior to the gospel in all its impartations of present and eternal blessedness. Here there is no poverty, no deficiency, no feebleness. In it are the riches, the perfections, the power of God. The forgiveness which it proffers is plenary, the spiritual enjoyments which it confers are unspeakable, the life which it secures is eternal. And that pardon, that joy, that eternal life are not the posted and ledgered dues for labor performed or services rendered, but the unmerited favors of infinite mercy and love—the gift of God through Jesus Christ our Lord.

In the gospel feast, all things are prepared by the King of

heaven, and the sinner furnishes no part of the entertainment. In accepting the divine invitation he has but to comply with the established usages of the banquet and enjoy the rich provisions so bountifully supplied. But oh! how often do the proud and the rebellious attempt to intrude themselves in contemptuous neglect of the appointed rules of decorum and without the robes appropriate to the occasion. How prone is the perverse and stubborn heart to betray its vain self-will by presuming to modify or disregard the arrangements of the Most High. And how often does the thankless hypocrite assume a seat at the festal board for base and selfish ends, without the least perception of the spiritual nature of the repast or the slightest relish for the "true bread of heaven."

It is that spiritual discernment, that earnest desire possessed by the true believer, which ever leads him to these blessed sources of spiritual enjoyment. It is because he is thirsty for the water of life that he approaches these living fountains. It is because he hungers after righteousness that he seeks this celestial food. He needs no artificial stimulants to quicken his spiritual appetite, and desires to mingle no foreign ingredients with the heavenly manna by which alone he lives forever. That blissful enjoyment which God himself has connected with the use of the means of spiritual life, wherever spiritual health exists, will ever lead him to the divine repast by which the soul is invigorated and refreshed. And that infinite perfection which everywhere marks the arrangements for the salvation of men will secure the accomplishment of every divine purpose and the fruition of every glorious hope.

12

"The Lord is in his holy temple;
the Lord's throne is in heaven;
his eyes behold, his eyelids try the children of men."
Psalm 11:4

How various and how pressing are the wants, real or imagined, of our poor fallen human nature. How earnest and how clamorous the appeals of the world. How engrossing and how harassing the anxieties and the labors they occasion. And how artificial and frivolous are the chief enjoyments of society.

Alas! it is seldom that the human heart is satisfied with the necessary blessings of life or content with the simple provision which nature demands and true religion warrants. The manifold lusts of the flesh are ever seeking new gratifications. The eye of Fancy ever roves abroad to discover unknown charms. The pride of life ever fills the soul with fresh ambitions and with novel fantasies. How difficult for the Christian, commingling in the cares and labors of the world, to escape its entanglements. The fashions of the hour, the gaieties, the amusements, the follies of life seek constantly to intrude themselves into the best-ordered household. The fondness of natural affection, the yielding temper of marital love, the ceaseless pressure of surrounding example, at once conspire to ensnare and overcome Christian principle, and often succeed in filling the home of the righteous with many unwanted cares and fears and burdens—diverting the attention from the things of eternity and piercing the heart with many sorrows.

Oppressive toils imposed by the tyranny of fashion enslave each member of the family and leave little time for pious meditation. The exacting demands of a transitory and selfish world forbid the delightful charities of the religious life. The nightly amusements, dissipations, and vain enjoyments of giddy youthfulness replace the once sweet time of family devotion and the hours of needed rest, while, amid the hurrying vortex, conscience remonstrates and piety pleads in vain.

Still, amid its trials, may the burdened soul live on, ever hoping for relief from its unprofitable toils and every refusing to yield up the hopes, the joys, and the precious promises of the gospel. Still may the heart desire to seek the Lord where he may be found, to draw near to him while he is near, to wait before him in his sanctuary, and to renew once more the spiritual blessedness of the past. How delightful the privilege to be permitted here to withdraw the mind for an interval from the bustle and the unsatisfying pursuits of the passing world. How sweet the moments which may be thus redeemed from the fast-fleeting hours of this vain and mortal life.

Surely, then, it is on this solemn occasion that we should

endeavor to draw nigh to God that he may draw nigh to us. Surely, it is here that these sacred memorials of a Savior's dying love should bring us into a peculiar nearness to our Lord. It is here that Jesus is set before us in his sufferings and death for the sin of the world, and that we appear before him as those who by faith have been made partakers in his salvation. Are, then, our hearts prepared for true and blessed communion with Jesus? Have faith and hope and love been aroused to lively exercise? Do we come with earnestness, sincerity, and penitential tears to the foot of the cross? Do we long in prayerful hope that the blessed vision of redemption may be unfolded before our eyes?

As Jesus came into the world for judgment and as he shall judge us at the last day, so, most assuredly, is he here to judge us now. Do we realize that it is with his all-seeing eye upon us that we are counseled here to examine ourselves that we may not eat and drink that condemnation which he awards to those who partake unworthily? Do we come with minds preoccupied and hearts unmoved by the momentous significance of the fact which we commemorate? Has the light of heaven been shut out and does the darkness of the world still brood upon our souls?

It is here, even amid this darkness, that faith may reveal to us the scenes of Calvary, that our world of earth-born cares may be shaken as by an earthquake, and the flinty rocks of our insensibility be rent asunder, and that we may be enabled to realize that this was truly the Son of God. It is at this hour that the veil which conceals from us the inner sanctuary may be torn away in order that we may behold the glory of the Divine presence. It is here we may revive the recollections of the past and bid the burial-places of memory give up their dead that we may go with them even into the Holy City. It is here that Christ himself may commune with us and that our hearts may burn within us while we gain larger views of the mystery of redemption and comprehend what the prophets have spoken of the sufferings of Christ and the glory that should follow. And it is here, above all, that the films of error may be taken from our eyes that we may recognize the spiritual presence of our Savior and that he may be made known to us in the breaking of bread.

How precious, then, this opportunity! How divine that bread of heaven of which, if a man eat, he shall live forever. How glorious the hopes which this blissful fellowship inspires. How sweet the peace which it diffuses over the soul amid the turmoil of life. How true a foretaste of that rest which remains for the people of God, that inheritance of eternal joy and blessedness which awaits the heirs of salvation.

13

"God is the Lord who hath showed us light:
bind the sacrifice with cords even to the horns of the altar."
Psalm 118:27

There is presented to our natural vision no difference so great and striking as that between the heavens and the earth. The little child, even, who sports upon the green and culls the familiar flowers of early spring, gazes with mysterious awe into that azure expanse so bright and pure, filled with the dazzling splendors of the sun or darkening with the approaching tempest. The thoughtless youth, reveling amid the well-known scenes and pleasures of life, grows serious for a moment when he surveys the unmeasured space where worlds unnumbered roll and shed their distant light. How bold and clear the line which marks the boundary of earth. How dense the mists that can obscure it. How dusky and opaque those rugged mountains which seem to serve as the abutments of the heavenly arch of azure light. How different in materials, how opposite in character, how unlike in every feature the earth beneath us from the heavens above. However great the differences of earth's varied scenes around us—of field and forest, of hill and valley, of land and water—their boundaries are dim and indistinct compared with that so deeply and abruptly marked by the dark line of the horizon.

But Nature not only distinguishes with striking clearness the things of earth from those of heaven, but teaches us by experience also that other precious lesson, that "every good and perfect gift cometh from above." From thence flow light and life with all their joys. Innumerable and mysterious influences thence irradiate the earth and grateful showers descend to bless the fruitful plains; and thither, too, all beautiful objects tend. Each tree and shrub and flower lifts itself aloft from the dark clods of earth towards the bright and glorious sky, as though it desired to approach the unwasting fountain whence it derives its being and its beauty.

In all these respects, as well as in others, "Nature is Christian—preaches to mankind," and seems to emulate in clearness the teachings of that divine word, which distinguishes the world and the things of the world from the spiritual heavens and the things that are of God, and which counsels us to "seek those things which are above, where Christ sitteth on the right hand of God," and to place our affections upon these.

Surely it is impossible to confound the glorious realities of true religion with the fleeting vanities of life. How plain the landmarks! How broad the distinctions! How evident the line which separates them! How unlike the one to the other in all that gives character and identity! Darkened, indeed, by the mists of error must be the vision which is unable to descry the spiritual horizon or to distinguish the bright and beautiful realm of life and glory from the dark and dreary abodes of death and shame.

But oh! how important that in distinguishing we should place our affections upon the things that are above. If the fair living forms of perishable matter that spring from the earth beneath may rise up to meet and enjoy the solar rays that vivify them, how should not they who have "tasted that the Lord is gracious" be lifted up above the world and approach nearer and nearer to that "Sun of Righteousness" whose beams impart unfading beauty and eternal life. How should not we seek the things that are above, where Christ sits, in whom our life is hid, from whom our life proceeds, with whom are all our hopes, our treasures, and our joys.

And how shall we direct our love toward that realm? How shall we disengage ourselves from our attachments to the world? Not by willing it, not by desiring it. We love not at our own pleasure, we acquire not by a wish. If the light of the glorious gospel of Christ has shone upon us; if its heavenly influences have revived us; if we have arisen from the dust of error's death and our hearts have been opened to receive the holy impressions of divine truth, then shall we be drawn by irresistible attractions, and strengthened more and more by added grace to ascend above the world and to approach the bright source of being and of blessedness.

It is by dwelling upon the glorious image of our Redeemer; by maintaining inviolate our relations with that "Eternal Life which was with the Father and was manifested unto us"; by cherishing that divine communion by which our souls are nourished, that we shall be filled with light and life and love, and become participants of that glory upon which we gaze, heirs of that life by which we live, and indwellers in that love through which we love.

And it is now, when we are thus assembled to commemorate what Christ has suffered for us, that we realize the most intimate relations of the spiritual life. It is when he is thus set forth crucified before us that he should command our homage and our affections. It is when he is thus "lifted up" upon the cross that he should "draw" all hearts to himself. Here, then, shall we dwell upon his love; here consider that life whose loss we celebrate; here rest in that sacrifice which reunites us to the divine fellowship and opens to us the fountains of celestial joy.

Happy they who are permitted thus to approach to behold the glory of God in the face of Jesus Christ as he appears in his holy temple, and to dwell in the house of the Lord forever. Who can behold without loving him? Who can love him without joy? We set our affections upon things above when we place them upon Jesus. These are where he sits at the right hand of God. He is "our Life." "Our life is hid with him in God." He is our Hope—"the hope of glory"—our "unsearchable riches" and our everlasting bliss. In him alone "wealth, honors, pleasures meet." With him is the "hidden manna," "the white robes of saints," the palm of victory, the "morning star" of praise. With him is "power, and riches, and wisdom, and strength, and honor, and glory, and blessing." In him all things are our own—whether past, present, or to come—the world, apostles, prophets, imprisoned death, emancipated life—since we are his and he is God's.

Holy and happy are they who in his blood have washed their robes. They shall be "before the throne of God and serve him day and night in his temple, and he that sits upon the throne shall dwell among them. They shall hunger no more, neither thirst any more; neither shall the sun light on them, nor any heat. For the Lamb which is in the midst of the throne shall feed them and shall lead them unto living fountains of water, and God shall wipe away all tears from their eyes."

14

"Thou art near, O Lord!
and all thy commandments are truth."
Psalm 119:151

How precious, how beautiful is truth. How worthless, how injurious, and how deformed is error. And how singularly has the beneficent Creator formed our nature that we might be able to discriminate between them. Whether it respects the objects of the material world around us or the more refined and mysterious things of invisible thought, how wonderfully has he provided us with powers of examination and of just discernment.

How quick and accurate is the sense of vision in discovering the presence and character of objects. How delicate the power of hearing! how discriminating the taste! how sensitive the nerves of smelling! and how reliable the information of the touch! Yet, however extended the range, however accurate the perception of each sense, the Creator has not restricted us to a single one. We might have been endued with the power of vision only or with that of taste or touch alone, and have been left to judge by its unaided power of every thing presented to us—to test thereby our food and poison, our safety and our destruction. But God has furnished us with five distinct and peculiar tests to determine the qualities of things; and, in his infinite wisdom and goodness, has endued those objects which are useful or necessary to us with qualities which delight the senses, while poisonous and unwholesome matters are gifted with properties which disgust and offend them.

Hence it results, as a general rule, that everything fitted to give us sensitive enjoyment is, within its appropriate limits, equally adapted to nourish and maintain us. These are the good things of animal life, analogous to the truths of the intellectual and moral nature—physical adaptations imparting at once pleasure, life, and health to the physical nature, just as moral truths give happiness and vigor to the moral constitution.

And what are all the varied attributes of mind with which we are endowed but so many tests by which we may discriminate between truth and error—the truth that saves, the error that destroys the soul? What are our powers of apprehension, our faculties of comparison, our attributes of reasoning and of judging but means of investigation and safeguards against delusion? And what that cautiousness in regard to our decisions—that disposition to pause, to hesitate and consider, by which the mind is characterized—but the outpost of the soul to prevent surprise, the indispensable precaution amid surrounding evil and aggressive error?

When, then, we consider the care which the Divine Being has manifestly taken to furnish us with ability to detect that which is injurious to us and to discover that which is conducive to our well-being—when we reflect upon the complicated nature of the delicate organizations through which he has thus sought to secure us against imposition and provide us with the good and truthful things of the natural as well as the spiritual world, how important must appear the right employment of these faculties and how valuable the objects they were designed to accomplish. And when we think of the superior nature of the immortal soul and the irrevocable and eternal destiny that awaits it, how incalculably precious must that sacred truth appear by which that soul is saved from ruin, and how dreadful the error by which it is deluded and destroyed.

It is here in the solemn teachings and institutions of our religion that this truth is presented to our contemplation. It is here, apart from the vain world in which the soul languishes, that this divine truth may invigorate the heart with the joys of a divine nature and diffuse through all its recesses that celestial peace which the world can neither give nor take away. For it is here that the King of saints himself provides the feast for his redeemed and satisfies the hungry soul with the bread of heaven and the water of life. It is here that He who is emphatically "the way, the truth, and the life" becomes himself the spiritual repast that yields eternal blessedness and supplies the welling fountain that springs up to everlasting life.

How pure the blessings which this truth confers! How sweet the liberty with which the Son of Man emancipates the soul! How glorious the destiny to which his love invites us! All other truths are precious, more or less, but this is a priceless pearl. All other truths confirm and strengthen one another, but this connects and corroborates them all. Without this, all else were vain and futile—the earth abortive and man himself an enigma and a failure. With this, the very mysteries of nature are unfolded, the dark places of the universe are lighted up, and consistency, wisdom, order, harmony, and love are seen to pervade the past, the present, and the future.

With what ardent desire, then, should the soul seek this ever-living and life-giving truth. With what readiness should it part with all that earth holds dear to secure the possession of this inestimable boon. And with what earnestness should it devote its powers and energies to the discovery and appreciation of that truth which is at once its light and life, its peace, its glory, and its joy.

But the truth that is so precious is not abstract or indefinite truth. It is not a mere mental conception—an unreal or ideal generalization. Nowhere in the Book of God have we any revelation of this character—any truth that is not eminently practical. If it be stated that "God is spirit," it is that he may be worshipped in spirit. If we are informed that "God is love," it is that we may be influenced thereby to love one another. If it be announced that "God is light," it is that we may walk in light as he is in the light. And if he be revealed to us in Christ as "the truth," it is that we may so receive him into the soul and banish thence the false idols of sensuality and corruption.

Christ is indeed "the truth," since he is "the brightness of the Father's glory and the express image of his substance"—"God manifested in the flesh"—"the only begotten of the Father, full of grace and truth"—"Immanuel, God with us." He is "the truth," as opposed to Satan, the father and the impersonation of falsehood. He is "the truth," as the fountain of salvation—the "author and the finisher of the faith." The Gospel is "truth" because it brings tidings of him. We are "in him that is true" when we are "in Jesus Christ"; and we "know the truth" when we know him and realize that he is "the liar who denies that Jesus is the Christ."

Especially here, in partaking of the mystic symbols of that sinless sin-offering upon the Christian altar, should we endeavor to appreciate the value of that sacred truth by which we live, endeared by dearest ties, approved by loftiest reason, received by living faith, and confirmed by an experience of the divine grace. That truth which came from heaven and thither reascends shall bear to the bosom of the Infinite those who have been purified by its love, while all who refuse obedience to its authority and walk in the broad road of error shall descend to the dreary abodes of death where their night of ignorance and crime shall be deepened in darkness by the storm of divine wrath and aggravated in horror by the hideous presence of Satan and his malignant hosts and the never-ending terror of eternal retribution.

15

"With thee is the fountain of life:
in thy light shall we see light."
Psalm 36:9

We are here convened to dwell on themes of deepest moment, to engage in heavenly ministrations, and to redeem a few sweet hours from the evil days of earth's corroding cares. How sacred the moments which are thus ransomed through the divine and pervading efficacy of the name of Jesus—of him by whom we are ourselves redeemed from death and ransomed from the grave. To him may they each one be consecrated. To him may each one bear the tribute of its praise.

It is here that solemn thoughts become us. It is here that soul-absorbing themes await us in the vestibule of heaven to lead us to the inner temple of the divine abode. It is here that we are presented with the memorials of that death omnipotent which has doomed the grave itself to desolation and forever abolished the domination of the powers of darkness. It is here that we are permitted to approach that perennial fountain of love from which we derive eternal life.

How solemn should be our thoughts of futurity. How serious our communings with the unseen world to whose eternal shores we hasten. How mysterious the gloom in which it is enshrouded. How eventful the moment when that gloom shall vanish from before the unsealed vision of the soul. Surely that approaching future may command our soberest thought and claim our deepest and most strict regard. Surely its immutable decisions may well engross the hopes and fears of deathless beings awakened to the dread realities which Truth reveals.

Who can contemplate the dissolution of the material frame without emotions? Who can meditate upon the inevitable hour of death and prepare to resign this pleasing, anxious being without one longing gaze of fond remembrance? But ah! if death be momentous, how much more solemn is the thought of life. How much more serious the reflection that we live—that we are raised from the senseless dust to breathe the vital air; to gaze upon the works of God; to hear his words; to move and act and feel; to realize that we are oral and responsible beings, that our every word and action is chronicled in heaven and every thought reported by an unseen but unerring stenographer of the soul. Ah! no; it is not death, the sleep of mortality; it is not the calm and dreamless repose of the tomb nor peaceful rest in the bosom of Abraham from the sorrows of the world that may be truly deemed of serious moment in comparison of life.

Yet ah! how few there are who truly realize the dread mystery of life and the momentous character of its eternal results. How many sport with time! How many waste away the sacred hours of life in thoughtless levity or in the dreamy stupor of unawakened ignorance and unconscious guilt.

Salutary may be the repose of the body, but the sleep of the soul is fatal. And ah! how often does the soul sleep—exposed, unwatched, and undefended—to become a prey to the spiritual assassin or a hapless prisoner manacled with fetters of dark despair. How often does even the Christian slumber, lulled by the treacherous cup of earthly pleasure and insensible to the life and light and joy of that divine radiance which shines forever in the blissful realms of the King eternal, immortal, and invisible. How important then the admonition to those that wake, to watch and pray lest the sleep of the soul should steal upon them and steep their spiritual sensibilities in lethal oblivion; and how appropriate to each of those who sleep, the solemn call: "Awake thou that sleepest, and arise from the dead, and Christ shall give thee light!"

16

"O Lord, how great are thy works!
and thy thoughts are very deep."
Psalm 92:5

How wonderful are the divine arrangements in nature and in grace. How overwhelming the grandeur of conception, the loftiness of purpose, and the infinitude of power, wisdom, and goodness manifested in God's dealings with man as his Creator and Redeemer. How mysterious the might by which he brings extremes together and compels them to succeed each other by a charming series of gradations, or to unite in harmonious actions, or even to produce each other. Day subsides into night, life leads to death: again, night gives place to day, and death to life. It is God who bends into the graceful ellipse of the planetary orbits the right lines of the two great opposing forces of the universe. It is God who, in the beginning of his creation, brought light out of darkness and it is he who will bring good out of evil in the closing triumphs of the great plan of redemption.

Among the singular incidents of human history which tend to illustrate this divine prerogative, we note that Satan, the apostle of death, is made to be the first preacher of life and glory. It was he who first announced to man that sublime revelation: "Ye shall not surely die; but ye shall be as gods, knowing good and evil"—a revelation which, though indeed false in its primary intention, is rendered most true in fact by the divine power in the Gospel of Jesus, who correspondingly says of those who shall obtain that future world: "Neither can they die any more, for they are equal unto the angels, and are the children of God, being the children of the resurrection." And surely the redeemed shall be, in one sense, as gods, being the children of the Most High, the brethren of Christ, knowing good and evil—not, indeed, as at first, the knowledge of good lost and evil got but now that of evil lost and good obtained.

Again: it is in harmony with the divine procedure that, as man died by eating, so it is by eating that he shall live forever. "I am the living food," said Jesus, "which comes down from heaven. If any man eat of this food he shall live forever, and the food that I will give is my flesh, which I will give for the life of the world." "As the living Father hath sent me and I live by the Father, so he that eateth me, even he shall live by me." The literal truth of Eden has its counter-sense in the spiritual truth of Christianity; and, as the mortal taste of the forbidden fruit brought death to the world, so a participation in the heavenly food presented by the Gospel communicates the enduring vigor of eternal life.

It is to partake of this tree of life of God's true paradise that we are here invited. How rich are its twelve-times varied fruits. How potent the virtue of its healing leaves by which the deadly wounds which sin has inflicted upon the nations may be forever healed. How glorious a privilege that we are thus permitted to become partakers of Christ, and to live by Him who died that we might live and rose that we might reign.

Yet it is not alone in the sanctuary of God that we are admitted to this privilege; nor is it alone in the divine institution of the Lord's Supper that we eat the flesh and drink the blood of our Redeemer. It is here, indeed, that, by these sacred emblems, we can most easily realize the figure in which Christ thus represents himself as the source of the spiritual life; but it is in the meditations of the heart in night-watches; in humble submission to the divine commands; in trustful reliance upon divine promises; in every exercise of faith; in every emotion of Christian love; in every act by which we enjoy communion with Christ that we receive him as "the heavenly food that gives life to the world," and, renewing our fainting energies, are enabled to toil onward and upward to the better land.

It is especially amid the abodes of sorrow and in the dark hours of affliction that we are likely to be found nearest to the "man of sorrows and acquainted with grief." It is not in the mansions of the great and the opulent, not in the festal hall of dissipation, nor in the proud palaces of kings that we are likely to find the humble Nazarene. But it is amid the disappointments of life; in the days of mourning and of desolation; in the hours of self-abasement and penitential love that we meet with Jesus. It is in the home of poverty and in the lowly mansion of the wretched that we may have fellowship with Christ. It is in the garden, not of delights, but of anguish—in Gethsemane, whose soil is watered with his tears and with his blood, or upon the bare and rocky mount, extended upon the agonizing cross, that we may find our Savior.

It is here that we are called upon to contemplate that divine love that was stronger than death. It is here that the dying sinner is permitted to look upon him thus lifted up, that, believing, he may have life through his name. It is here that all may approach him in humble adoration and yield the soul captive to the conqueror of death and the grave, who has triumphed for us over all our enemies and is become our light and life, our hope and our salvation.

17

"He made darkness his secret place;
his pavilion round about him were dark waters
and thick clouds of the skies."
Psalm 18:11

Christianity deals not with trifles nor was the mission of
Jesus for unimportant ends. The subjects and the purposes which are here presented to our view are, on the contrary, of the deepest moment and of the most absorbing interest. Rejecting the vain objects of the fleeting world and all the idle themes which pertain to earth, the Gospel embraces the things of life and death and, entering at once upon the stern realities of human destiny, dwells on those solemn truths which, from their very nature, are fitted to engross the attention of every human being.

Yet life and death, the great themes of religion in which man is so deeply concerned, are among the great mysteries of the universe. How little we know of life, although it is everywhere around us and even within us. How much less we know of death, of which we have had as yet no personal experience. Doubtless, however, it is this very obscurity which gives to these subjects an interest so deep and permanent. What we have fully explored and comprehended wearies us by familiarity and loses its attractive charm. But mystery awakens curiosity; engages attention; excites inquiry; gives activity to thought and zest to enjoyment. How just, then, that the most important things should be the most mysterious. How proper that we should be thus led to dwell upon these with fixed attention. How fitting, also, that we should be most deeply interested in the things which Christianity presents. Nature attracts us by the wonders of a life and a death which are temporal, but religion enchains the soul by the deeper mysteries of a life and a death which are eternal.

In proportion as the mysteries presented to us deepen they approach nearer to God. He is the great mystery of mysteries, and we draw nearer to Him as we approach the veil that conceals the sacred arcana of his inner temple. Life natural is to us a great enigma, and it reveals to us much of all that we yet know of God; but death, that still greater mystery, will open to the soul still nearer views of God in the world of spirits.

In our investigations of nature, we may trace effects to their immediate causes and discover important truths in regard to the divine system of material things. It is when we would seek to explain and analyze these causes themselves that we find ourselves involved in deeper and more remote researches, and it is then, when we approach the mystery of the divine will, that we are brought nearer to the invisible Creator. It is untrue, then, that a mystery that is truly divine can obstruct our progress or hinder our vision. On the contrary, it tends to give us truer and nobler views of the Deity because it brings us nearer to Him and yet veils, in a favoring obscurity, that dazzling glory which would otherwise blind our feeble vision.

Thus it is not the light of day that gives to us the most glorious and sublime view of the material universe. We then see the earth beneath us and the vast expanse above us with its single sun on which, from its very brightness, we dare not gaze and whose very light conceals from us the rest of the material system. It is when that light is withdrawn and darkness casts her sable mantle over the things of the earth that our view, instead of being contracted, is enlarged and fixed upon the heavens. It is then that worlds upon worlds arise before us and millions of suns appear in place of one, and distant and still more distant orbs lead us farther and farther through the regions of illimitable space to the unresolved nebulae of utmost vision; to the sublime mysteries of nature; to the overwhelming grandeur and magnificence of the divine creation; to the infinite power and glory of the Creator.

So, also, though life reveals much of God to man, it is death that shall unfold much more. It is the night of death, the darkness of the grave, which, while it hides from us the earth, shall reveal to us the heavens and display to the soul those sublime mysteries of Deity which, though now above us and around us, are yet concealed from us by the very brightness of our day of life.

But what is true of our own life and death is eminently so of the life and death of Jesus. How great was the mystery of the life of Christ! How thick the veil in which the divine glory was then enshrouded! Yet it was thus alone that man was enabled to approach so nearly and to contemplate so fully the glory of the Only Begotten of the Father, full of grace and truth. It was through that mystery of the incarnation that God was indeed revealed to mortals. It was amid the darkness of the world that his infinite love, mercy, and condescension shone forth to the view of men.

But ah! how much greater the mystery of his death! and how much more it presents to us of God! What new and wonderful developments it gives of the divine character. What awful and sublime conceptions of the Infinite One it presents to the soul. What startling thoughts it suggests of the things invisible. What sorrowful memories of the past; what blissful fellowship of the present; what joyous hopes of the future cluster in the broad heaven which the death of Christ reveals.

Ah! it is here that we see more of God than angels knew before! It is amid the darkness of the grave of Jesus that new visions of God arise, more sublime and glorious than all that could precede. It is indeed the bright light of His presence that dazzles and blinds. It is light that renders Him inaccessible, so that no man can approach Him. It is into the thick darkness that we must enter, like the leader of ancient Israel, if we would find Him. It is when He shrouds his glory in the veil of mortality; when He partakes of our deep woes and enters into the gloom of our dark and dreary prisons that we may presume to draw near to Him in trustful faith, to enter into a holy spiritual communion, and partake of the ineffable joys which wait upon his presence.

18

"The Lord of hosts is with us;
the God of Jacob is our refuge."
Psalm 46:11

How frail and weak is human nature! Born into the world a helpless infant unable to provide for its humblest wants, it is only through the assiduous care of others that man can at all be preserved in life. A mother's gentle breast must nourish, her hands protect, her thoughtful mind provide for and supply her feeble charge. And oh! how long, and through what anxieties and fears, what dangers and what toils, must parental care lead the tottering steps of childhood and the thoughtless inexperience of youth up to the years of maturity and reflection. Even then, with all his boasted powers, how dependent is man upon his exterior sources for sympathy, encouragement, and support. Rejoicing in his fancied strength and esteeming nothing impossible to his efforts, he yet finds that alone and unaided his strength is but weakness and discovers that it is necessary to lean upon others, and to merge his fragmentary being in the strong and lofty edifice of society, to which he may impart, while from it he hopes to receive strength and elevation.

But even here, environed by all the aids and sympathies which spring from the natural or social relations and friendships of human life, how deeply the thoughtful mind must realize man's native feebleness in the dark seasons of unrequited toils, of disappointed hopes, of unlooked for and irretrievable calamities—when the world reveals its nothingness and the heart despairs of heaven and no human agency can afford relief. And still more, when life wanes amid its cares and is ready to perish with the perishing things which have occupied its busy hours—when man grows old and "his strength faileth," when the faculties of mind and body have become enfeebled, and childish fancies and dim memories return along with the tottering steps of infancy in old age—and most of all, when the hour of dissolution comes and no mortal skill can alleviate or remedy the suffering that must be endured alone—when every power that life and nature gave is wholly lost—when the eye is glazed and sightless, and the ear no longer hears the voice of affection, and the hand returns no more the grasp of friendship: oh! it is then that the heart may truly realize the utter feebleness and frailty of human nature, the emptiness of all its claims, the nothingness of all man's worldly hopes.

In taking part of flesh and blood, Jesus partook of our infirmities and bore our weaknesses as, in his own body, he bore our sins. It is not in his maturer years merely that we are to behold the man Christ Jesus. It is not through fanciful speculations concerning his natural endowments or his human motives; or in seeking to be wise above what is written of his spiritual conflicts, that we are to contemplate or to comprehend our blessed Lord's humanity. It is rather in the feeble infant in its unrocked cradle, the helpless Christ-child, nurtured upon a mother's bosom or hastening to her side with pattering feet for protection or for solace; it is amid the growing years of youth and all its trials, winning divine and human favor by meek submission and by cheerful aid; it is in the fulfillment of his sacred mission, as a homeless wanderer, in weariness and want, a gentle minister of grace and peace and truth, sympathizing with human suffering, partaking of human woes, and enduring the contradictions of the ignorant, and the contumely of the proud—above all, it is when, finally, through the eternal Spirit he offered himself without spot to God as the propitiation for our sins—it is in that supreme hour, when faint but firm, he experienced for us the bitterness of that death in which all human weakness has its consummation, that we may contemplate aright the Blessed One who became our kinsman that he might be our Redeemer.

Had he not assumed our nature, he could not have borne our griefs or carried our sorrows. Had he not become a partaker of flesh and blood, he could not, through death, have accomplished our deliverance and destroyed the dominion of him that had the power of death. That mighty work was not completed until the last agony was endured, the last loud cry was uttered, and the expiring lips had pronounced the verdict, "It is finished," as he bowed his head in death and hung motionless and pale and cold upon the bloody cross.

He was, indeed, "crucified through weakness," yet it was in that moment of extreme weakness that he gained the victory. What neither the divine law, nor rich oblations, nor human power could do was accomplished in the death of Jesus. God's weakness is stronger than men, and He who has constructed the lofty mountains with grains of sand and with drops of water the boundless ocean has ever chosen weak things to confound the mighty and the lowly to abase the proud. Through his "foolishness," so much wiser than human wisdom, he has reconciled us to himself by the death of his son, in vindicating thereby the inviolability of the divine justice and rendering the divine mercy accessible to the believer. "What shall we say, then, to these things? He that spared not his own Son, but delivered him up for us all, how shall he not with him also freely give us all things? Who shall lay any thing to the charge of God's elect? God that justifieth? Who is he that condemneth? Christ that died, yea, rather, that is risen again, who is ever at the right hand of God, who also maketh intercession for us?"

Hence it is that with love's memories of the past we can blend the joyful hopes of the future, and thus continue to celebrate the death of Christ until he come. For he it is that lives and was dead; and behold, he is alive for evermore and has the keys of death and hades. And surely, "if when we were enemies, we were reconciled to God by the death of his Son, much more, being reconciled," shall we be "saved by his life." If the rich boon of forgiveness and gracious acceptance is accorded to sinners, oh, how untold and inconceivable the blessings that are prepared for saints! If, in the weakness of humanity, Jesus could accomplish the mighty work of reconciling the world through death, how much more shall he not now save the reconciled with an eternal redemption by the power of an endless life.

Since it is in death that all human weakness culminates, it

is in life that strength divine resides; and if, in the weakness of death, he has destroyed the dominion of sin, shall he not in the strength of life secure victory over the grave? If while on earth, straitened in the shackles of mortality, "crucified through weakness," he overcame the powers of darkness, how much more now, that he lives by the power of God, shall he not come in the glory of his Father and with all his holy angels to obtain an eternal redemption for us. It is then, indeed, that the last enemy shall be destroyed; that this natural body which is "sown in weakness, shall be raised in power"; that "this mortal shall put on immortality, and death shall be swallowed up in victory."

19

"Out of Zion, the perfection of beauty, God hath shined."
Psalm 50:2.

How treacherous is the darkness! How full of ambushes!
How fearful in its terrors, its dangers and its crimes!
How useless the keenest vision amid its rayless gloom. How
unavailing in its entanglements and struggles of human power.
How secret too are its approaches. How silently at eventide,
when

> The trailing garments of the Night
> Sweep through her marble halls,

does she steal forth to pursue the retreating footsteps of the
day. With faltering pace and shrinking fear, she follows in the
distance, seeking the shelter of each shadowing object, creep-
ing along the eastern mountain slope or reaching forward
beneath the dusky mantle of a favoring cloud.

How she shuns the high summits where the sun's bright

banners continue to float, and seeks to gain the victory, not by brave assault, but by cowardly stratagem. And how do her dark legions tremble and retire before even a straggling parting ray from the western heavens?

Light, on the other hand, how aggressive! How quickly at the reveille she marshals her forces and speeds across the vast abyss of space upon her mission of glory. How speedily she puts to flight the powers of darkness. With what rapidity she assails their fortresses and their towers. With what facility she surmounts their bulwarks, levels their defenses, exposes their secret machinations, discovers their ambuscades, and reveals their guilt. How she sheds brightness and beauty over the earth, where brooded the blackness of darkness and despair. How she opens the prison-doors, breaks the chain of the captive, and replaces the silence and the desolation of death by the joyous songs and blessed activities of life.

It is thus, in the moral world, that the sun of righteousness shines forth out of Zion upon the darkness of the soul. "God is light and in him is no darkness at all." And it is from the mount of his holiness, from Zion the joy of the earth, that he sends forth the light of life. It is here he displays his power and glory. It is here he has "commanded the morning" and "caused the day-spring to know his place." From here he has ordained that his arrowy rays of light shall "take hold of the ends of the earth" to put to flight the hosts of darkness. Here is known "the way where light dwelleth," and here alone are the "paths to the house thereof." For the church of God is the "light of the world." To it are committed those precious oracles which alone can illuminate the dark places of the earth and to it appertains the mighty work of spreading abroad the life-giving truth— "the grace of God which bringeth salvation."

How sad the condition of a world lying under the dominion of the Prince of Darkness. How feebly we may realize its sorrows, its sufferings, its hopeless despair. How imperfectly we may comprehend its mysterious enigmas or by human reason explore the secrets of its wretchedness. How vainly seek relief for its miseries in the impotency of man's devices. And oh! how great that sacred trust, that priceless boon—the divine commission which alone can open the blind eyes and turn men from darkness unto light and from the power of Satan unto God, and which God has given into the hands of his people. What duties, what responsibilities are theirs in presence of the awful facts of the present and of the hastening future. How deeply should they meditate upon the obligations which rest upon the church as the pillar and support of the truth.

How appropriate that in this hour when these sacred memorials are before us and that precious sacrifice which takes away the sin of the world is set forth in these expressive symbols, that we should dwell on the unspeakable gift of God and ponder the lessons which it teaches. Have our own souls been clothed with the light of its truth? Have our hearts been divinely impressed with its significance? Has our nature been renovated by its power and clothed with the beauty of holiness? Are we walking in light as the children of light? And, in fulfillment of our mission, are we reflecting that light upon others and striving to dissipate the ignorance and darkness of the world?

Are we seeking to rescue helpless victims from the debasing slavery of sin? Are we, in imitation of our Divine Exemplar, laboring to destroy the works of the devil, to expose the mysteries of iniquity, to raise the fallen, cheer the faint, support the feeble, and diffuse the glorious light of the Gospel throughout the abodes of ignorance, superstitution, and cruelty?

Alas, how many there are who fail to fight the good fight of faith! How many who obstruct the progress of light and truth! How many who mutiny against the captain of salvation! Else why have we around us these battalions arrayed against each other? Why these different standards, these opposing counsels, these conflicting orders? Why do the mists of error which the night has gathered conceal true allies both from each other and from the sunshine of heaven? Why these party names, these unkind dissensions, these rivalries and ambitions? Where is that concentration of resources which can alone supply the means of warfare? Where is that unity of power which alone can give victory?

Surely it is the hour when the followers of Christ should awake from the lethargy which ages of darkness have imposed. Surely it is time that all who have entered into His holy covenant should hearken to his voice and assemble themselves together for the great final conflict of righteousness and truth.

It is here within these sacred precincts that we should realize that divine spiritual unity which can be preserved only by the bond of peace. Partakers of one bread, we are one body. Animated by one Spirit, cheered by one hope, led by one Lord, sustained by one God and Father of all, it is here we should ever feel the eternal ties which bind us to each other. It is here amid the light of life and the joys of salvation that we may renew our vows of fealty. It is here we may put on the armor of light and prepare to contend together "against principalities; against powers; against the rulers of the darkness of this world; against spiritual wickedness in high places." It is from the heights of Zion we must go forth, marshaled beneath the banners of our heavenly King, in compact array, aggressive, invincible and victorious, to scatter the legions of darkness and fill the earth with the glory of the Lord.

20

"The heavens shall praise thy wonders, O Lord;
thy faithfulness also in the congregation of the saints."
Psalm 89:5

It is in the sanctuary of God that the mystery of man's condition can find its only interpretation in the wonders of redemption. It is here alone that light dawns upon the night of the grave and that the enigmas of a present world and of a mortal life, at once so sweet and sad and strange, can be to any extent resolved. It is here that an inscrutable Fate which, like the fabled Saturn, seems to destroy its own offspring gives place to a beneficent Power, gathering the harvests of Time into the garners of eternity and selecting from the nurseries of earth those flowers which may fitly bloom forever in the gardens of heaven.

It is here that order is imparted to a seeming chaos; meaning and purpose to an unintelligible maze; dignity to debasement; power to weakness; wisdom and goodness to seeming

unprofitableness and decay. It is here too amid these wondrous lessons that man discovers his own inefficiency and
learns to trust, in trembling hope and humble adoration, an
over-ruling and Infinite Intelligence.

It is hence here in vain that carping unbelief may seek to
awaken dubiety or fear through those uncomprehended facts
of the present which pertain to the unrevealed secrets of the
future. However mysterious the controversy between good
and evil; however varied the fortunes of the struggle; however
protracted the toils and sufferings of the righteous or boastful
the transient triumphs of the ungodly, it is here that an assured
faith preserves in perfect peace the heirs of salvation, the called
according to the purpose of Him who works all things after the
counsel of his own will.

It is hence here that the disappointments of life, the failure
of fond human hopes, the complications which often enshroud
in obscurity the plans of Providence, disturb not an equanim-
ity which reposes upon the Divine faithfulness; and though the
seeds of truth may often be scattered upon the waste places of
the earth to yield apparently no genial harvest, though the
brightest and the best may be prematurely snatched away or
the cherished objects of affection be ensnared by the Tempter
and dragged to endless ruin, there still remains the blessed
assurance amid all the dimly comprehended problems of the
present that the eternal God is our only refuge and that
"beneath are the everlasting arms."

Amid the inscrutable mysteries of nature, the pious heart
humbly rests secure in the infinite wisdom and goodness of an
Omnipotent Power who fills the universe with created wonders in munificient profusion, and imparts the charms of life
and beauty to myriad forms of dependent beings, each perfect

in its sphere and tributary to the grandeur, the glory, and the completeness of the whole. Nor, amid the still greater mysteries of religion, does the renewed soul fail equally to humble itself before the unsearchable judgments of God and, encompassed with the doubts, the fears, the oppressive secrets of human life and destiny, to accept in joyful confidence the guidance of Divine truth.

It is hence here that to hearts beleaguered within the narrow walls of sense, Faith, like the swift-winged passenger-dove, brings blessed messages from the distant and unseen world to enlighten and to cheer. How joyful these news of approaching deliverance! How sweet these assurances of triumph! How absorbing these intimations of intended movements, these glimpses of ulterior purposes. Involved in sin and sorrow, mortality and death, by one man's disobedience, we learn that by the obedience of one we shall be ransomed from the power of the grave, and that "as by the offense of one, judgment came upon all men to condemnation, even so by the righteousness of one, the free gift came upon all to justification of life." If hence, sin has reigned unto death, righteousness shall reign unto eternal life, the Omnipotent One having provided for every woe a solace—a balm for every wound.

How glorious is the Divine scheme of redemption! How potent and far-reaching those agencies which countervail the pervading virus of evil which flows onward in the life-current of our race. What world-wide oppositions! What wondrous analogies and resemblances! If the first Adam gave rise to sin, the second Adam brings in an everlasting righteousness. If the former brought death upon the world, the latter brings life and immortality. If, in the one case, the innumerable offenses of many supplemented the disobedience of one—in the other, the obedience unto death of one, singly and alone, secured for all the free gift of justification.

It were, however, to conceive unworthily of this glorious salvation to esteem it merely the counterplot or counterpoise of sin, and to imagine that, with this, the redemption which is in Christ Jesus forms but an equation whose members are equal to each other. While, with our feeble powers, we may not essay to sound the depths of that vast deluge of suffering with which sin has overwhelmed the world or estimate aright either the malignity of its nature or the eternal consequences which result from it; nor, upon the other hand, form any adequate conception of those gifts of grace and blessedness which God has prepared for those that love him, we are nevertheless divinely assured that the work of Christ is not a mere antagonism to sin, a mere neutralization of its power and its effect, a mere restoration to a precedent condition.

Ah! no; in the infinite purposes of Jehovah a nobler, mightier consummation is designed. It is here that the eternal is to replace the temporal; the spiritual, the carnal; the Paradise of God, the earthly garden of Eden. It is here that the most precious and beautiful things of earth can be but types and imperfect emblems of the unfading glories of the future, and that the divine promises shall confer a "far more exceeding" weight of endless bliss than sin had here ever exacted of suffering and affliction.

Whatever, in the decrees of a just and holy God, may be the significance of the symbolic pictures of the Apocalypse or of the brief literal announcement of "everlasting punishment," or an "everlasting destruction from the presence of the Lord and the glory of his power," as the doom of the finally impenitent; however deep and awful may be the meaning of the

announcements, both of the privation of good and of the infliction of evil, in which the wicked shall share with those malignant spirits who left their first estate and seduced man from his
allegiance, it may not be affirmed that the penalties of retribution shall bear an exact proportion to the rewards of the righteous, or that the unmerited gifts of grace shall be bestowed
upon the redeemed in equal measure only with the merited
anguish of the lost. It is in the dispensation of blessedness that
a beneficent Deity, with whom judgment is "strange" and who
takes no delight in the death of the wicked, has imposed upon
himself no limitation, but reserves for the righteous the highest joys, honors, and dignities of heaven, exalting them to the
heirship of all things and to the participation of infinite delights
adapted to new and enlarged capacities of enjoyment.

If sin, then, with its evils has abounded, grace with its blessings has much more abounded. If death, in all or any of its
forms, has reigned by one, much more they who receive abun-
dance of grace and of the gift of righteousness shall reign in life
by one, Jesus Christ.

How precious, then, in the sweet hours of sacred meditation these simple but expressive memorials of that death which
brings to us more than life—of that humiliation which has
exalted humanity to the throne of the universe. How dear to
the heart are those yearnings of faith and love which here
bring us near to him who has washed us from sins in his own
blood. And oh! how bright, amid the darkness of the world
and all the sad mysteries of sin, that light of eternity which
here illumines the pathway of the just.

21

"Be not conformed to this world: but be ye transformed
by the renewing of your mind, that ye may prove what
is that good, and acceptable, and perfect will of God."
Rom. 12:2.

There is but one true religion; all else are counterfeit. There
is but one religion that can take a man to heaven; all others
are useless. And the religion that can take a man to heaven
is a religion that renders him fit for heaven. For heaven itself
would be a place of punishment to those who were unfit for its
society and averse to its enjoyments; and a religion would be
justly discredited that promised admission to a state of perfect
holiness and happiness, and yet had no obvious tendency to
prepare man for that condition.

Man is made fit for heaven by being restored to the divine
image, favor, and fellowship. A religion that does not do this is
but an empty profession. All true religion leads to fellowship
with God. Satan destroys man only by separating him from

God. All pain and sorrow are in this, and the judicature of heaven knows no higher punishment than "an everlasting destruction from the presence of the Lord and from the glory of his power."

It is much to be feared that this great object of religion is overlooked by many of those who make a profession of Christianity. How often this seems to be regarded merely as a system of redemption or salvation. How often it is looked upon from a selfish point of view, as something which a man may add to his other possessions; as something which may be acquired, like property, for private and personal advantge. How often it is conceived to be something which is offered to men as a commodity, which they may obtain upon certain terms, of which the ministers of the Gospel are supposed to be the negotiators.

But Christianity is very far from being a mere system of redemption from sin, or salvation from punishment, or selfish rewards for obedience. It designs not only to bestow remission of sins but to effect a renovation—a regeneration of the soul. Indeed, it is not too much to affirm that it can be a means of salvation only as it is a means of renovation—in other words, that no one can be saved by it who is not renewed by it. Hence, no one can be truly said to possess himself of religion since, on the contrary, it is religion itself which takes possession of man, and "in Christ Jesus" nothing is of the least avail but "a new creature."

The person thus renovated is a spiritual one. He is "created anew in righteousness and true holiness." He is "God's workmanship, created in Christ Jesus unto good works." He is a living temple for the indwelling of the Holy Spirit, which is to him the earnest of a spiritual inheritance—the antepast of an eternal reunion with God.

Yet how many there are who seem to have no such conception of the nature and intentions of the Gospel; who are but spots in the divine love-feast of Christianity, clouds without rain, trees that bear no fruit, failing fountains which mock the thirsty traveler. They profess to follow Christ but in works deny him. They are sensual because they have not the Spirit and, like those who partook of the loaves and fishes, seek Jesus from selfish motives, indisposed to receive his spiritual instructions and ignorant of the nature of his reign. Those declarations which are the most precious to the sincere believer are to them "hard" sayings which they can not hear and which, if forced upon their attention, will speedily expose their true character and designs.

How great a master of the heart was Jesus, who could thus detect and exhibit the false zeal of selfishness and disperse the thronging multitude of seeming friends. How pertinent the question to the remaining few: "Will ye, also, go away?" How unavailing the ready sponsorship of Cephas with him who knew that, even among those selected by himself, there was one betrayer.

Many, indeed, are called but few are chosen in the dispensation of the Gospel. The good seed of the heavenly kingdom fall often on uncongenial soil, where it finds no depth and can establish no permanent relation. How many who seem to enjoy great privileges here will fail to be acknowledged in the day of the final account by him who weighs the actions and appreciates the motives of men. It is not a mere verbal acknowledgment of the Lordship of Jesus nor, as many seem to suppose, a mere connection with his church that will take a man to heaven. An outward union to the church is indeed an important movement—it is one step on the way; but heaven is too high—it needs more than one step to gain it.

Some seem strangely to imagine that it is only the grosser and more public vices that religion proscribes. They appear to think that a Christian may cherish envy and avarice in his heart; that he may live at variance with his neighbor and suffer anger to rankle in his bosom, and yet continue within the pale of salvation. They distinguish sins into venial and moral, and suppose that strife, enmity, and uncharitableness are really less offensive to God than robbery and murder. They themselves fear and abhor the thief and the assassin because they have something to lose by them, and think that the Divine Being will regard them with the same feelings of displeasure and look, as they do, with greater allowance upon the person who secretly envies or hates his brother. They forget, however, that to him who looks upon the heart, anger and avarice are the real crimes—the very causes which lead to those consequences so much more criminal in the sight of men. They are ignorant that the works of the flesh—the workings of the carnal mind—are all alike hateful to God, who needs not to await the overt act before he ascertains the secret character, and with whom no outward decency of behavior can cloak the moral turpitude of the soul.

It is not mere formal adoration of a carved, a graven, or a molten image that constitutes idolatry. On the contrary, it is the giving the heart's affections to any thing that is not God. Any thing may become an idol except God, and he only is free from idolatry who loves the Lord his God with "all his heart, and mind, and soul, and strength." "Alas!" cried the leader of Israel, "the people have sinned a great sin, and have made unto them gods of gold." What matters it whether it be a golden calf or a golden eagle, if it usurp the place of Him who should be the delight of the soul, the charm of the heart, the lord of the affections and desires? He who enshrines the passion of avarice in his bosom is as great an idolater as he who bows before the hideous image of Vishnu; yet the crime of covetousness, like that of witchcraft, seems to be unknown in modern days and to have wholly disappeared from the revised codes of ecclesiastical discipline.

But the Christian is one who has "renounced the hidden things of dishonesty," and has no desire to avail himself of the license afforded by modernized Christianity. His divine code of morals tolerates no "fashionable vices" and permits no venial crimes. Renovated in heart, he "purifies himself from all filthiness of the flesh and spirit," and "perfects holiness in the fear of the Lord." Influenced by the sublime motive of love to God and strengthened with all might by the Divine Spirit in the inner man, he triumphs over the world and its allurements, and enjoys a celestial purity and peace which the world can neither give nor take away.

Doubtless there are many who make a vain profession of the Gospel. Actuated by a transient sympathy, a momentary impulse; driven by fear or attracted by visionary hopes, they become ostensibly members of the Church of Jesus Christ, yet remain forever ignorant of the "power of godliness" and strangers to the "faith that overcometh the world." Like the flying fish that springs from the briny wave with glittering scales to sparkle for a moment in the solar rays and sink again from view into its original and proper element, so do these heartless professors, for a brief period, appear in the sunlight of the Gospel, only to return immediately to their natural and appropriate place—the world.

But the course of the true believer is like that of the passenger bird which sets forth to seek a more congenial climate. It pauses not upon its journey, except to gather the simple food which is necessary to subsistence. It stops not to spend the precious hours in bowers of love, but speeds its lofty flight, with wing unwearied, until it has reached the peaceful regions where it can find secure repose.

The Christian religion, in short, proposes nothing less than an entire transformation of the human character. This must be accomplished or there can be no well-grounded hope of future bliss. It is not by the establishment of mere formal or ceremonial relations with the Deity or with the Christian Church that this is to be attained. True relations, indeed, exist only as effects or consequences of a change of heart. And these are not mere abstract relations but true relationships.

Among men we have often true relationships where we have no family resemblance, as where children are unlike their parents. But in the spiritual world we can have no true relationship without likeness. The pure in heart are related to each other because they are alike, and they are related to God and will be admitted to his presence because they resemble him. It is not the space between heaven and hell that separates the righteous from the wicked, but their contrariety of character and their alienation of soul.

How true it is, then, that only by a conformity to the divine character men can become partakers of the salvation of God. How evident it is that only by a renovation of heart men can be prepared for heaven. He who seeks a foreign land will wisely learn its laws and language and provide himself with its current coin and secure to himself friends who will receive him there. How sedulously should the Christian, then, labor to render himself thus familiar with heaven and thus to furnish himself with such sterling attributes of character as are stamped with the image and superscription of Christ. How earnestly he should seek, by fellowship with God here and by keeping his commandments in faith and hope and love, to provide for himself friends who will receive him into the eternal mansions.

22

"Give unto the Lord the glory due his name:
bring an offering, and come into his courts.
O worship the Lord in the beauty of holiness:
fear before him, all the earth."
Psalm 96:8, 9.

How precious are the hours appropriated to the worship of the Most High. How soothing to the wounded spirit the sacred offices of religion. In the assembly of the saints a heavenly peace diffuses itself over the soul. Amid the solemn invocations of earnest prayer, the world and all its vanities disappear. Its corroding cares, anxieties, and fears are banished from the heart and replaced by freedom, joy, and blessed hopes. The swelling anthem of divine praise bears, upon wings of melody, into the deepest recesses of our nature the transporting truths of revelation, awakens the dearest memories of the past, or marshals in bright array the crowding visions of the future.

What thronging images cluster around the welling fountains of thought and feeling. How enrapturing these spiritual
delights which are the pre-libations of future blessedness.
How sweetly the responsive fervors of gratitude and love com-
mingle with the pensive meditations of penitence or remorse.
How clearly now are the secrets of the heart revealed before
the bar of conscience. How swiftly does busy memory recall,
in all its moral relations, the history of the past.

Where now are those once dearly loved with whom we held
sweet converse and communion—the friends of our youth,
now perhaps alienated or long forgotten? The tokens of affection unrequited, the consciousness of duties unfulfilled, the
remembrance of the dear ones who rest in the cold and silent
grave and to whom we may speak no word of regret and offer
no evidence of unchanged regard, are all strangely interwoven
with the deep joyfulness of the present and with the glad
assurances of an eternal reunion in the realms of glory. We see
them again in the visions of memory. We hear again their voices re-echoing in our hearts. We receive again their glances of
confidence and love.

But, ah! we long in vain to clasp the fleeting shades and to
confess how far we have failed to reciprocate their tenderness
or appreciate their solicitude and loving care. Amid the tumult
of our feelings, how sweet those tears which flow unbidden,
yet, ah! how unavailingly, save as they serve to reveal us to
ourselves, to chasten our affections and assure our hopes.
How delightful are those moments, rich in blessing, when the
soul dissolves, as it were, in a grief that is full of joy, in the consciousness it gives of the immortal nature and unmeasured
depths and capacities of our moral and spiritual being.

But, alas! for that apostate memory, that nature lost to love and truth, that here, in presence of these sacred memorials of a love which, as the sunlight hides the stars, obscures by its superior glory all mere human affections, may experience no remorse and realize no blessedness. These consecrated emblems speak to us of Him who has washed us from our sins in his own blood—of Him who, while we were yet enemies, has given himself for us that he might redeem us from death and ransom us from the power of the grave.

Alas! for the insensibility of this poor sin-stricken heart, for that paralysis of the inner nature which enfeebles and benumbs our spiritual powers. How often, alas! since that divine love was assured to us in the blest time of our espousals have we failed to fulfill our vows of faithfulness. How often have we forgotten the enduring constancy and unswerving truth and boundless love of our adorable Redeemer. How often have we become negligent of his instructions. How often have we rebelled against his authority. How often been ungrateful for his benefits.

And now he is presented here to us wounded to death in our behalf. That disfigured visage, that bleeding form so "marred more than the sons of men," those pierced hands which he had stretched forth only to bless, those beautiful but now lacerated feet which had borne him on his heavenly mission of love—here present themselves to the eye of Faith, and we seem to witness that now lifeless body, enshrouded in the habiliments of death and laid in the dark and silent tomb. Alas! shall those ears, once ever open to the cry of the suffering and the penitent, never more receive our words of sorrow and contrition? Shall those loving eyes never more welcome our return? Shall those divine lips never more greet us with the assurance: "Thy sins are forgiven thee"? Shall we never more renew the blessed fellowship of the past? Alas! how vain are tears of grief or words of penitence or promises of amendment when the grave has hidden from our eyes the neglected or the injured! How fruitless now are self-reproaches. How futile now the hope of renewing the sweet intimacies of friendship or of love.

But, oh! what startling revelation meets us here. "Now hath Christ risen from the dead and become the first fruits of them that slept." Shall we then, indeed, once more be permitted to behold him? Shall we again listen to his voice? Shall we again receive his favor and enjoy his presence? Assuredly not, if, with the eager haste of carnal doubt that trusts alone to sensuous proofs, we rush like Peter or John to gaze into the tomb of the crucified Redeemer. We shall perceive there naught but the cerements of the dead and shall return unblessed and unrewarded.

Oh! it is in these solemn moments when the seen seems to blend itself with the unseen, when Time merges into Eternity and Death resolves itself into Life, that the heart commands a solemn and a sacred pause. It is in this hour that we may stand in the stillness of trustful hope and in the conscious helplessness of our feeble nature to see the salvation of God. The spiritual perception of the soul requires the faith of the affections, the loving confidence of the heart, and it is with Mary we must remain in patient waiting for Jesus if we would indeed receive the joyful assurance of an angelic vision or be permitted to see once more in reality the risen Lord. Near as he was to Peter and to John, they saw, they heard him not; they trusted to their own perceptions; they relied upon their own understandings.

Oh! that we may judge not by feeble sense, but in faith and

love await our Savior. It is here he shall then meet with us to inquire: "Why weepest thou?" "Whom seekest thou?" It is here we may again enjoy our blissful communion as of old and hear his guiding words of truth and renew our vows of fealty. And it is here we shall be permitted to rejoice in the blessed assurance that, at the appointed time in the bright regions of eternal glory, we shall rejoin the loved and lost, where all sorrow shall be forgotten, all tears wiped away, all faithful love and fellowship be restored, and where, amid fullness of joy and spiritual blessedness, "we shall be forever with the Lord."

23

———

"The sting of death is sin; and the strength
of sin is the law. But thanks be to God,
who giveth us the victory through our
Lord Jesus Christ."
1 Cor. 15:56, 57.

How terrible is that malady which death alone can cure!
How irremediable that distemper whose termination
can be found only in the destruction of the sufferer! How mortal that evil from which there is a refuge only in the grave!
How sad that condition where all human appliances are vain,
where Life may linger without Hope, and consciousness
remain only to perpetuate despair.

Yet such a malady as this is sin, inherent in that carnal
nature, that depraved moral and physical constitution, that
"body of death" in which man is now condemned to fulfill
those years of penal servitude which precede the hour of his
inevitable doom. "For sin has entered into the world and death

by sin, and death has passed upon all men, for that all have sinned." The penalty of "capital punishment" has been announced against all by an infallible Judge whose sentence is irrevocable. Already, indeed, in its highest sense, has that dread sentence been fulfilled when man is left alienated and separated from God and debarred from those fountains of joy—that spiritual communion which alone can truly constitute the life and blessedness of the soul.

What varied means, what strenuous efforts have men employed throughout the ages in the vain hope of discovering for sin or for its effects an appropriate and efficient remedy. Philosophy has sought to lull the sufferer into a repose more cruel than wakefulness and vexed with horrid dreams. It has endeavored to benumb all sense, to steep the soul in forgetfulness, or soothe its fretful anguish by the fictions of the imagination. It would impugn the evidence of consciousness in asserting that "pain is not an evil," or in mockery tantalize the wretched victim burdened with the ills of mortality in declaring that "pleasure is the only good." It would seek to convert the object of sense into mere appearances and ideas into reminiscences of the real and eternal patterns familiar to the soul in a prenatal state of being, as emanations of that divine idea which alone exists. It has traversed the wide regions of speculative thought, but to end its fruitless search for truth and life in darkness and in doubt. A dying Socrates orders a vain oblation to an Esculapius incompetent to afford relief or rescue.

The greatest of modern philosophers announces that "the highest reach of human science is the scientific recognition of human ignorance" (Sir William Hamilton). There is here no real power to enlighten, no hope to cheer the desponding, no salvation for the lost. The mysteries of sin are here left unexplored, the secrets of death unrevealed, the light of life undiscovered.

Again have men supposed that in ritualistic observances, in outward forms, in the fulfillment of the ordinances and commandments of law they would be able to attain to righteousness and peace. But, alas! how unavailing is delight in even the divine law when opposed to that imperious "law in the members" which ever wars against the "law of the mind" and takes occasion by the commandment itself, which is holy, just, and good, to bring the soul into condemnation and captivity.

How feeble before the overmastering supremacy of the carnal nature is the human will. How fatally that commandment, which was ordained to life, becomes transformed into a ministration of death. How sin, by its very means, achieves its greatest victory and how futile is that mortal struggle when law itself imparts life and strength and malignity to sin, and, far from aiding in the conflict of the soul, serves but to aggrandize guilt and inflict the dread penalties of its own violation.

And yet, again, how vain have been the efforts of mankind to obtain deliverance through the sin-offerings whose blood has bedewed their altars. How essentially vain the knowledge that death alone could even typically save the sinner, since in the blood of the victim there was no meritorious efficacy, no power to purge the conscience, no life to energize the soul. What hecatombs have been vainly offered amid the rites of heathen and of Jewish worship. How unavailing have been all the penances of superstition, the oblations of idolatry, the self-immolations of fanaticism. Through what weary hours of darkness have men sought to find their way—groping after God if haply they might find him—and how fruitless has been their search for truth, for righteousness and life.

Yet, ah! how near to all has ever been the Divine presence and how long in patient love has the Almighty borne with man's apostasy and vain devices. How gloriously has he at length himself achieved deliverance and salvation through that righteousness which is "by the faith of Christ unto all and upon all them that believe." How freely is man justified by his grace through the redemption that is in Jesus, whom God himself has set forth to be a propitiation through faith in his blood, to declare his righteousness for the remission of sins.

Apart from all the avails of human wisdom and independent of all deeds of law, Christ has appeared in the closing age of the world to put away sin by the sacrifice of himself. Made of a woman, made under the law, he has expiated in our human nature, through the infinite purity and dignity of his own, the accumulated sin of this world. How truly in that Holy One who was in the likeness of sinful flesh, in that Divine Sin-Offering, has sin in the flesh received its condemnation. How fully has the just and holy law of God been vindicated and magnified. How wondrously has infinite justice been reconciled with mercy in this unspeakable gift of God.

How sweet in this hour the reflection that the work of Christ is perfect. Death has taken sin away from all who have died with Christ. With him the sinful nature is crucified that the body of sin might be destroyed; and, since he that is dead is freed from sin, sin may no more have the dominion. But it was not the mission of Jesus merely to overcome the Powers of evil and secure for us an escape from guilt and punishment. It was not merely to fulfill the requirements of the divine law and give freedom to the condemned, but to impart also light to the benighted, rest to the weary, strength to the feeble, and life to the dead. If, through Him, we are dead to sin, it is that we may be alive to God. If we have been crucified with Christ and through faith planted in the likeness of his death, it is that we should be also in the likeness of his resurrection.

As in that loud shout of victory which he uttered upon the cross, he announced his triumph over the malign principalities of the unseen world and, in that final moment, stripped off from himself those hostile spiritual foes who had ever sought in vain to seduce the human nature which he bore, so may the believer, through the death of Jesus, ever repel the Powers of darkness and overcome the temptations of the world. For in that death was destroyed him that had the power of death, and from the grave has Jesus brought again that human nature of which he is with us a partaker and over which death can have no more dominion. As, then, in that he died, he died to sin once but, in that he lives, he lives unto God, so may the Christian ever realize that he is "dead indeed unto sin, but alive unto righteousness through Jesus Christ our Lord."

24

"The Lord is my shepherd I shall not want.
He maketh me to lie down in green pastures:
he leadeth me beside the still waters.
He restoreth my soul: he leadeth me in the
paths of righteousness for his name's sake.
Yea, though I walk through the valley
of the shadow of death, I will fear no evil:
for thou art with me; thy rod and thy staff
they comfort me."
Psalm 23:1-4.

Multitudes of men have died, but only one Christ. All others died by sin, but he alone for sin. How wondrous is the nature of this death! How deep its significance! How vast its results! How far beyond the human faculties to invent a scheme of redemption of whose grandeur, even when revealed, man is unable adequately to conceive.

"Christ died for our sins according to the Scriptures." "He laid down his life for us." "He bare our sins in his own body on the tree." What transcendent facts are these! How full of meaning! How full of mystery! How full of the hope of deliverance! Is sin, indeed, put away? Is there pardon for the guilty and life for the dead? Has a substitute been found for the condemned to endure the penalty in his stead? Have the guilty been, indeed, thereby set free from the consequences of transgression?

If so, then why these fears, these pains, these sorrows of earth, these wars and fightings, these crimes and desolations? Why these funeral rites, these mourning urns, these monuments of death? Have the divine purposes been frustrated? Has Jesus shed his blood and given himself for the life of the world in vain? Ah! no; but man, untaught of God, ever conceives amiss of spiritual things and occupies himself with the visible and the temporal rather than with the unseen and the eternal. Unconscious of his true condition, he comprehends not the deliverance which the Gospel brings and, since it proffers not exemption from bodily suffering or from natural death, he regards it with indifference or rejects it with disdain.

How incorrect a conception, alas, it would be of the work of Christ were we to suppose that he came merely to prevent the enforcement of the penalties of sin by enduring these for us. How narrow a view of the efficacy of the Sin-Offering upon Calvary to imagine it merely a species of commercial substitution, an equivalent exchange, or the ground of mere juridical acquittal. Truly, the death of Christ of itself prevented the infliction of no penalty, compromised none of the eternal principles of justice, frustrated the fulfillment of no divine decrees. The world of the ungodly has still remained alienated from God by wicked works and "dead in trespasses and sins." Over all of Adam's race death has still reigned, alike over infant and adult, saint and sinner.

Far nobler, higher, better purposes were involved in the death of Jesus than the mere removal of the penalties of man's transgression. He came "to put away sin by the sacrifice of himself." He came "to destroy the works of the devil," to introduce a mighty era in the affairs of the spiritual and temporal universe, before which he was set forth as a propitiation to declare God's righteousness, that he might be just and yet the justifier of him that believes. This wondrous death affects not only the consequences of sin but sin itself. It relates not merely to Adam's fallen race, but reaches in its vast results to the unseen world, to the throne of the Eternal, to the moral and physical destinies of the universe. Through it is to be destroyed that mighty spiritual foe who has the power of death and who, with all his rebel hosts, shall be consigned to everlasting fire. Through it even the heavens and the earth shall be remodeled and nature itself readjusted to new conditions of glory and beauty.

Meanwhile, is it not true that Jesus "hath abolished death and brought life and immortality to light"? Has not the Gospel been preached to the dead? Have not they that were dead heard the voice of the Son of God and lived? Most assuredly has it been the work of Christ to deliver souls from death in this, its highest and truest sense—a death in trespasses and sins—a state of separation of the soul from the favor and fellowship of God. This separation he endured on our account—a separation which probably took place from the moment in which he was "delivered up by the determinate counsel and foreknowledge of God," and the near approach of which wrung from him the bloody sweat in the Garden of Gethsemane and the plaintive appeal: "O my Father! If it be possible, let this cup pass from me"; as well as that pathetic exclamation upon the cross: "My God! my God! why hast thou forsaken me?"

This was that veritable and awful death of which alone the patient sufferer complained and of which all other deaths may be considered but as symbolic or consequential—a death which had rested upon the whole human race since Adam by transgression fell, who, in the very day in which he sinned, was severed from the divine communion which he had enjoyed in Eden. Hence, the sacrifice of Christ could neither anticipate nor prevent the execution of this dread penalty which was already enforced. Deliverance from its power alone was possible, and this alone to those made conscious of their condition and willing to be freed.

Thus, though the Gospel be preached to the dead, it is only those who hear that shall live. For "faith cometh by hearing," and "God gave his only-begotten Son that whosoever believeth in him might not perish, but have everlasting life." The impartation of life here could not follow as a necessary consequence of Christ's assumption of humanity and his sacrifice for sin. A death that rests upon moral and spiritual causes can be replaced only by a life which equally springs from a moral and spiritual source; and where will may choose and responsibility exist, there only may such a death be suffered or such a life be given.

It is the individual, who through faith has become dead to sin, that is made alive to God through the redemption that is in Christ Jesus. On the other hand, it is he that "believeth not the Son" who "shall not see life" and upon whom the wrath of God shall continue to abide. How terrible that hopeless death which broods over the souls of the ungodly and culminates in "an everlasting destruction from the presence of the Lord and from the glory of his power."

But there is a death which Jesus died for man, of a different nature and followed by different results, so far as it relates to humanity in general, viz.: the separation of the body from the soul. This death was one of the consequences of man's separation from the Divine presence in Eden, when he was cut off from the tree of life and his bodily frame was left to exhaust its unrenewed energies through lapse of years and to return finally to the dust from which it had been taken. It is, then, to the frailty and perishableness of the body alone that this death is due. The soul itself knows no decay and neither needs nor desires to be unclothed. It is not the soul which abandons the body, but it is the tottering frame which, with enfeebled vitality and worn-out tissues, sinks into ruin and forsakes the soul. In the order justly indicated by the sacred penman, it is this mortal tabernacle which, by a necessity that is inevitable, is resolved into its elements while the freed spirit returns unchanged to God who gave it.

This death, too, Jesus could have experienced when his human life and human nature should have fulfilled the common destiny of humanity. But it was not permitted to be so. "His life was taken from the earth." In the full vigor of manhood and with all the years of maturity unspent, and all the latent energies of man's corporeal being yet unwasted, he gave his life for us and by cruel hands was crucified and slain. He endured this separation of soul and body by violence as the Divine Victim, "the Lamb of God" who should "take away the sin of the world."

It is this wondrous sacrifice which here, with appropriate material elements, we now commemorate. This bread is his body broken for us. This wine is his blood shed for us. As material beings we may learn, through material images alone, the deeper spiritual lessons of the world unseen, and these emblems, in imperfectly shadowing forth the crucifixion of Jesus, show forth a death which, however terrible, was itself but expressive of that more awful separation of the soul from God and those inexpressible and mysterious sufferings which he endured on our account. Nevertheless, as this bread and wine represent to us the body and blood of Christ, and in our hearts we should here behold him openly set forth crucified before us, so does the crucifixion of Jesus embody in itself to the world the entire sacrifice, the entire visible manifestation of the Divine Sin-Offering.

It is in this, then, that to us every thing is included; and, however justly the mind may frame distinctions or partially penetrate into the unspeakable mysteries of the death of Jesus, it is Christ and him crucified that alone should occupy our hearts and consecrate our lives. It was in his own body on the tree that he bore our sins. It was through the stripes inflicted upon him that we have been healed. It was upon the cross that he was made "a curse for us" and suffered in all their forms, however mysterious and manifold, the penalties of our transgressions.

Christ having, by thus "offering himself once for all," opened up a new and living way of access to God, it is the individual who accepts the Divine mercy and, abandoning sin, returns to God that is released from that penalty of spiritual death which rests upon the world. He was previously alive to sin and dead to God; but is now dead to sin and "alive to God through Jesus Christ our Lord," and can experience no more that death from which he has been freed. In this sense it is that "he that believeth can never die," that "he shall not taste death," that "he shall not see death." The Divine favor and fellowship shall be no more withdrawn, for the life of the believer is hid with Christ in God and there can be no more separation for those who have "put on Christ," who walk in him, who live by faith in the Son of God and are sealed with the Holy Spirit of promise—the earnest of an eternal inheritance.

But the Christian, like others, must still experience the separation of the body from the soul. From this the death of Christ has not released him, for this penalty is demanded in accordance with the inflexible decree of God and the unchanging purpose of him who has higher things in store for man than that he should dwell forever in the flesh. Hence, "it is appointed to all men once to die"; but oh, wondrous revelation! Since Jesus truly partook of our nature, uniting it with the divine; since he endured this bodily death also on our account and, having power to lay down thus his life and power to take it again, has accordingly renewed again the connection of body and soul, resuming that crucified form in which he suffered, so it is equally the divine appointment that all who thus in Adam die shall be made alive in Christ, and that this separation of body and soul shall also be terminated by a reunion.

There is this difference, however, that, as the death of the body is not moral or spiritual but natural and in harmony with the inflexible laws of the material system, not depending on choice or human will but necessarily affecting the entire race without exception, so the reunion effected in the resurrection of Jesus necessarily relates to all and results in the resurrection of all, not depending on human choice or will or any moral reason but taking place in virtue of the same inflexible divine purposes and arrangements which for sin had consigned all

men to the grave. As the first fruits give token that all suc-
ceeding plants of similar nature shall in like manner attain
fruitage and produce the ripe corn in the ear, so the resurrection of Christ as "the first fruits of them that slept" gives evidence that the resurrection of the body is the final ordination
of God, and that as Jesus is the "plague of death," so will he
be also the "destruction of the grave."

Hence, while in addressing the Jews in reference to that
death to God which rested upon men, he said: "The hour is
coming, and now is, when the dead shall hear the voice of the
son of God, and they that hear shall live," he presently added,
in relation to the death of the body: "Marvel not at this, for the
hour is coming in the which they that are in their graves shall
hear his voice and shall come forth—they that have done good
unto the resurrection of life, and they that have done evil unto
the resurrection of damnation."

How perfect, then, in power, how complete in fullness is
the work of Christ. How far-reaching the consequences of his
death and how glorious the salvation he accomplishes by his
life. How precious the assurances of his mercy, faithfulness,
and truth. How blessed the hope of his return. How fully has
he now taken away the sting of death and how sweetly he
"gives to his beloved sleep" during those peaceful hours which
usher in for them the bright morning of an eternal day.

For Further Reading

Selected Writings by Robert Richardson

Memoirs of Alexander Campbell. 2 volumes. 1869.

The Principles and Objects of the Religious Reformation, Urged by A. Campbell and Others, Briefly Stated and Explained. 1853.

A Scriptural View of the Office of the Holy Spirit. 1872.

"Faith versus Philosophy," *Millennial Harbinger* 4th series, 7 (1857). [The first of a series of 8 articles published in 1857 and 1858.]

"Nature of Christian Faith." *Millennial Harbinger* 4th series, 6 (March 1856), 153-60.

"Nature of the Christian Doctrine." *Millennial Harbinger* 4th series, 6 (April 1856), 198-204.

"Pure and Undefiled Religion—No. 1." *Millennial Harbinger* 5th series, 2 (November 1859), 622-26.

"Reformation—No. IV." *Millennial Harbinger* 3rd series, 4 (September 1847), 503-509.

"Union of Christians." *Millennial Harbinger* 37 (March 1866), 97-101.

Selected Writings about Robert Richardson

Allen, C. Leonard. "Unearthing the 'Dirt Philosophy': Baconianism, Faith and the Quenching of the Spirit." In *Things Unseen: How the Theology of Churches of Christ Brought Success in the Modern Age (and Why After Modernity It Probably Won't)*. Forthcoming.

Allen, C. Leonard, and Danny Swick. *Participating in God's Life: Two Theological Crossroads for Churches of Christ*. Orange, CA: New Leaf Books, 2000.

Brooks, Pat. "Robert Richardson: Nineteenth Century Advocate of Spirituality." *Restoration Quarterly* 21 (1978), 135-49.

Goodnight, Cloyd and Dwight E. Stevenson. *Home to Bethphage: A Biography of Robert Richardson*. St. Louis: Christian Board of Publication, 1949.